The Fenghuang and Dragon Motifs in North America:
A New Perspective of Western Hemisphere Pre-Columbian History

Jon R. Haskell

Indigenous Peoples Research Foundation

Parson's Porch & Company

Parson's Porch Books

The Fenghuang and Dragon Motifs in North America: A New Perspective of Western Hemisphere Pre-Columbian History

ISBN: Softcover 978-0692465349

Copyright © 2015 by Jon R. Haskell

All rights reserved. No part of this book may be reproduced or transmitted in any form or by any means, electronic or mechanical, including photocopying, recording, or by any information storage and retrieval system, without permission in writing from the publisher.

To order additional copies of this book, contact:

Parson's Porch Books
1-423-475-7308
www.parsonsporch.com

Parson's Porch Books is an imprint of Parson's Porch & Company (PP&C) in Cleveland, Tennessee. PP&C is an innovative non-profit organization which raises money by publishing books of noted authors, representing all genres. All donations from contributors and profits from publishing are shared with the poor.

The Fenghuang and Dragon Motifs in North America:
A New Perspective of Western Hemisphere Pre-Columbian History

Introduction

Universally found symbols have long been a subject of debate. One position argues they are a result of independent development and the other, a result of cultural migration. In this paper I argue for the later position by presenting a gallery of tracings of subtle background motifs now known as the Chinese Fenghuang bird pair and a believed to be pre-Neolithic Dragon depiction on various venues including: lithic tools, sculpted heads, figurines, caves, escarpments, stone tablets, buildings and silk monochromatic paintings from both hemispheres.

The graphics will illustrate that the motifs first appear on Solutrean lithic material and remained generally unchanged in appearance and positioning relative to each other to later in time Clovis examples from the Cactus Hill and Gault sites in North America, and the Neolithic site of Laonainaimiao in Henan Province China. T

More recently in history, I present a sculpted skull from Chavin de Hunatar in Peru dated 1500 BCE bearing the two motifs and which also has diagnostic elements of the Mesoamerican rain gods Chaac and Tlaloc, along with other Mesoamerican examples showing the motifs continued use on Olmec thru Aztec artifacts.

Focusing on cultural groups in eastern North America and the upper Ohio River Valley, I present tracings showing the continued use of the motifs by the Paleo-Eskimo in the Sub-Arctic to the more southerly Glacier Kame, Adena, Hopewell and Mississippian cultures.

As an art based research project, this paper is heavily graphic dependent with limited commentary, but it will demonstrate that the world has always been a small and there is much to be learned about the history of the Western Hemisphere.

In 2014, an amateur surface collector chanced across a 30cm Chinese votive sword partially exposed in an eroded creek bank in the northern part of the State of Georgia, USA. Fashioned from Lizardite, the exquisitely carved sword has a host of diagnostic Chinese symbols and motifs, the earliest of which are attributable to the Shang Dynasty (c 1556-1046 BCE). Near the sword, amongst the rock rubble of the creek bed, two pristine Olmec-style face pendents were found. At another location ten miles distant from the sword, other seemingly out of place artifacts were found, including a greenstone squatting figurine with possible Finno-Ligric based script[1] spanning it's elaborate head dress.

It was during pedestrian surveys of these location, the two unfamiliar motifs were first noticed. They appeared in great quantity on rocks ranging in size from small two inch hand-held pieces to a fifty foot plus monolithic sized rock fashioned into a bird shape. Initially, the motifs were thought to be unique to

---

1 Stuart Harris and Michel J. Boutet, papers located at www.precontact.org

this region and possibly associated with Mesoamerican groups. This was based upon the Olmec-style face pendents, numerous parrot or macaw shaped stone bird effigies and familiarity with literature regarding this probable interaction scenario. Adding to the ambiguity was the Chinese votive sword with zoomorphic depictions of Taotie and other Chinese symbols. Incrementally it became clear that the motifs were based upon the Chinese Fenghuang and Dragon.

To demonstrate my findings, I present a gallery of tracings from the various locations, time periods and venues which are representative of a larger group of tracings. Also included are artifacts that have a controversial background and along with some that are personal favorites because of their uniqueness.

Photographs were analyzed using ImageJ software with the DStretch © color stretching plug-in. Tracings are based on a synthesis of: pecked and linear incised tool marks, naturally occurring fissures and contours, color differentiations produced by image software, familiarity of repeatable artistic conventions learned over time, and bird anatomy. It is assumed the figure outline marks on the bronze, crystal and silk examples were the result of the "outline and color" method using paint or in, because the use of a hard tool seemed out of place for the medium.

Extrapolation was used sparingly and thus many outlines and specific features are incomplete because of uncertainties. Tracings are minimal with the hope that the features they are based upon are evident to the reader, however the illustrations to do not compare in detail to the results from a high-resolution monitor.

Compounding the difficulty associated with producing accurate tracings, is the density and layering of motifs found on the examples. For example, there are routinely two or more bird eyes clustered in close proximity indicating multiple heads of different sizes sharing the same space and having beaks in different orientations or a smaller beak sharing a portion of a larger beak.

Dragon symbols are also layered on top of each other, each appearing in various orientations and sizes making it nearly impossible to identify which facial feature goes with which face. Not all motifs on a object are traced to avoid a cluttered appearance. Thus, though considerable time and care was taken in the tracings, there are undoubtedly errors in tracing, but do not detract from presence of the motif.

Descriptions and Observations of North American Motifs

Paired-Bird Motif or *Fenghuang*

One of the birds in the pairing is interpreted as a parrot or related species based upon it's distinctive beak and rounded head, along with the overall body shape in side profile. Tool markings identifying the beak can be quite obvious and surprisingly anatomically accurate. Tool marks forming a "U" shape indicates an open beak.and provides a reference to identify the lower margin of the top beak and the top margin of the lower and smaller beak. In many cases however, heads of various sizes occupy the same space with beaks in a different orientation or a smaller beak part of a larger beak. making identification of which beak goes with what head difficult if not impossible.

The other bird character has a long and slender beak with a slight downward turn at the end and a more slender body. While such a general description could apply to a number of species, the Raven or Crow seem probable candidates given their global role in ancient mythologies. They along with the parrot can serve as an avatar for the sun or the sun itself.

As a general rule, the eyes of the parrots are formed by two pecked concentric circles, which is also a diagnostic element in Mesoamerican art for the Macaw eye. Long beaked bird eyes seem to be formed with a single pecked circle, however in some cases the eye cartouche is oval shaped with pointed ends. Invariably, there will be cluster of two or more eyes in a small area which obviously indicates multiple birds and tracing difficulties.

The type of bird can be determined by the line that delineates the beak and the head. If the line is curvilinear and located adjacent to the eye, the bird is a parrot. On a long beaked bird, this line is located further from the eye and not curvilinear.

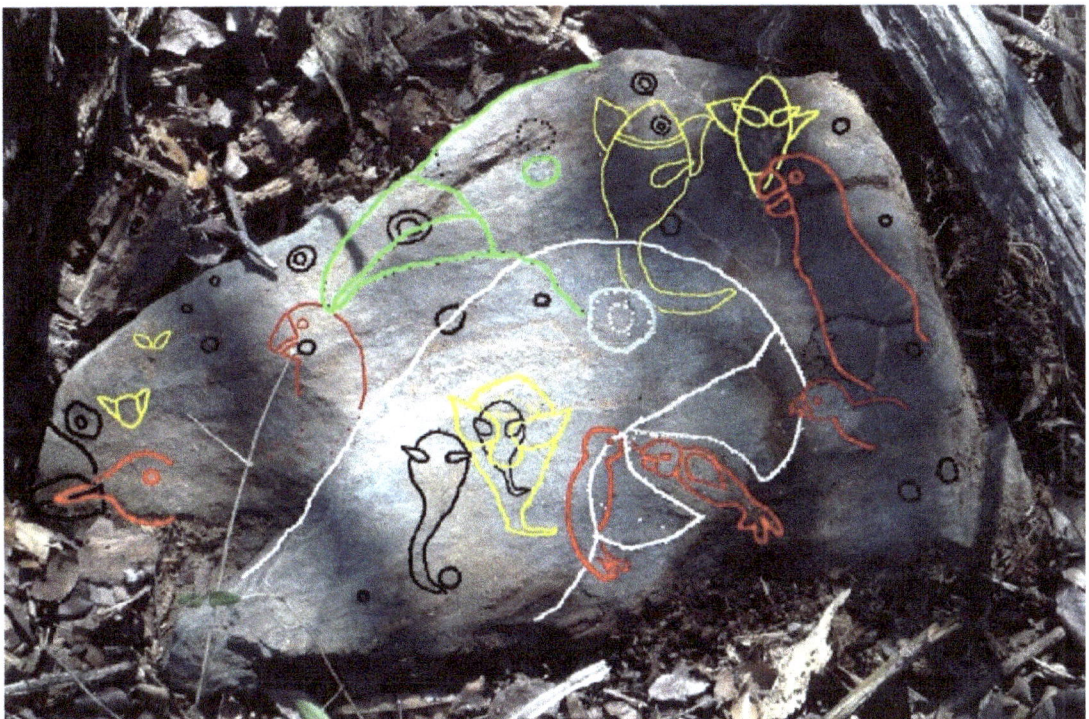

Fig.1, Bird Head Rock, showing birds, dragon-faces and bird eyes, Georgia, USA, by author

No attempt was made to quantify the use of one bird versus the other, however subjectively within the many examples reviewed, the parrot seems represented by a overwhelming margin. It would be an informative exercise to quantify bird type by region and mythology globally.

The juxtaposition of paired bird beaks varies. The long beaked bird variations include: close, tips touching, overlapping forming an "X", parallel to each other, and occasionally appearing to be inserted into a parrot beak. Parrot beaks are normally positioned close or touching each other. In many cases, the parrot beaks are open and "holding" an object.

Birds are normally displayed in side profile, however the heads are occasionally depicted as viewed from the front. In the lower right of figure 1 are two identical eyes with an unmarked beak achieving this perspective.

I was continually amazed at the density of images on an object. and the cleverness of the artist(s). To illustrate, figure 2 is from a small area below the long green beak shown in figure 1. Circles indicate bird eyes interspersed with the ever present dragon. I have purposely left some bird eyes and dragons unmarked to give the reader the opportunity to find them.

Conflating images within one motif or between both motifs is common and include: forming a smaller bird from the wing of a larger bird, sharing a portion of a motif's outline, dragon-faces used as bird eyes, the horn/wing of a dragon as bird beak. One of many unanswerable questions is if the symbols were created at one time or added overtime.

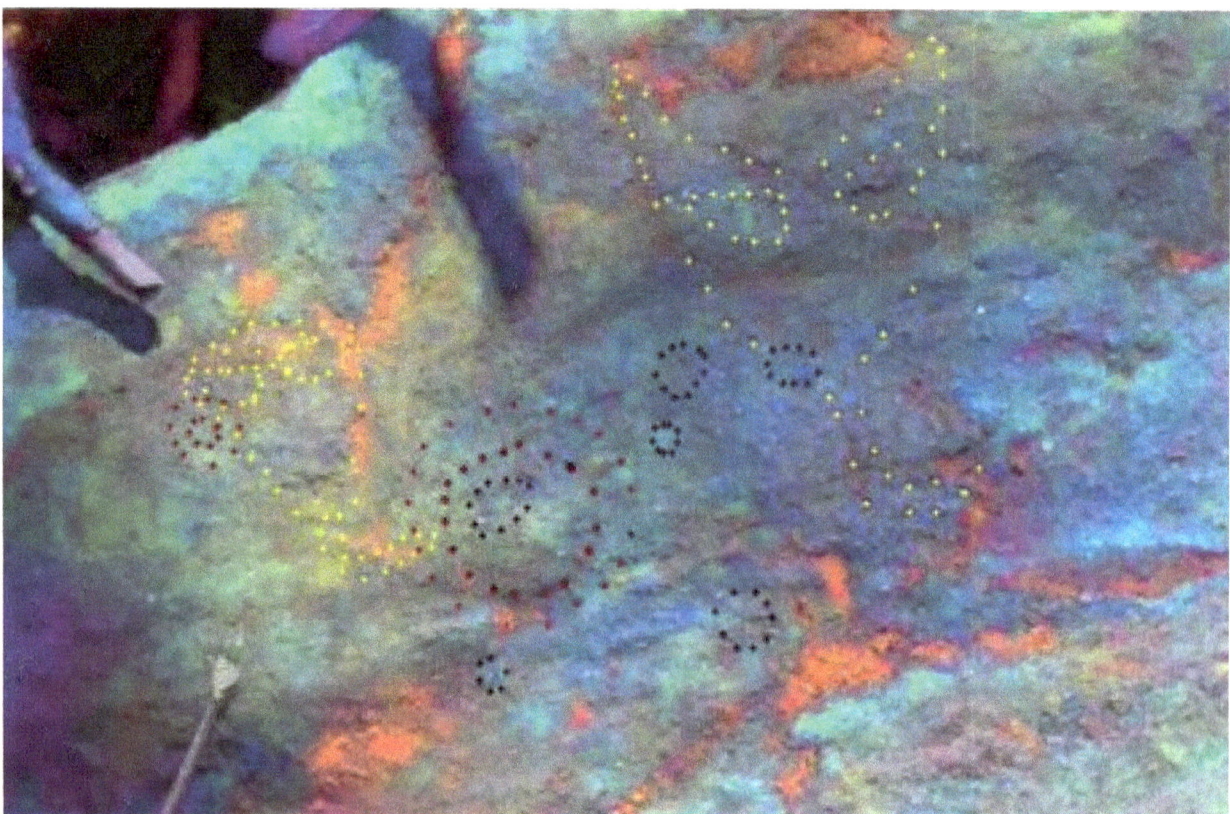

Fig. 2, Close view of bird shape rock, Georgia, USA, by author

Dragon Motif

There are two diagnostic elements that make presence of the dragon symbol visually apparent. First, the shape of the distinctive upward slanting almond shaped eye cartouche stands out in the maze of other visual information. The shape of the eyes stylistically do vary slightly, but retain the upward slanting pointed appearance and extend to the edge of the head (figures 3,4)

On larger examples, there can be a double-line eye-brow motif starting between the eyes following the eye contour and many times appear to extend beyond the head forming a flattened "V" shape. Many times there is a small feature on the forehead which produces a different color when viewed in color stretched images. The nose, which is rarely discernible, is bulbous and pear shaped. On some larger examples you can identify a double-line feature spanning the forehead creating a headband appearance.

The perimeter of the head can generally described as skull shaped with the lower one-third, or "jaw" area, narrower than the upper area. They also can appear more triangular in shape with two triangular "horns" and occasionally having a pointed "cone-head" shape. Wing, and horn elements are curvilinear and end in a point. Some wings are quite long, starting in the jaw region and gradually expand in size. These head features are noticeable because of their shape, however are difficult to assign to a particular head for reasons explained next.

It is difficult, if not impossible, to trace an individual face with a high degree of certainty because they are always layered on top of each other. Each face, seemingly in a cluster of three or more, will be slightly different in size and with a slightly different orientation making following tool marks to determine which facial feature goes with a particular head problematic. The layering also makes it difficult to discern a matching eye which is illustrated in many of my tracings with only one eye. These difficulties can be seen in figure 4.

The number of dragons at any location can be determined by the number of tails below the heads. Like eyes, the tail motif is very noticeable within in a maze of other tool marks. The lines forming the outline of the tail start just above the bottom of the head. gradually narrow, travel vertically, and then normally veer to the faces left. Many times you get the impression that the tails are segmented with horizontal lines. On large rocks along water ways, the tails will go to great lengths to reach the water line.

Fig. 3, Sculpted head, dragon motifs, Manchester, KY USA, by author

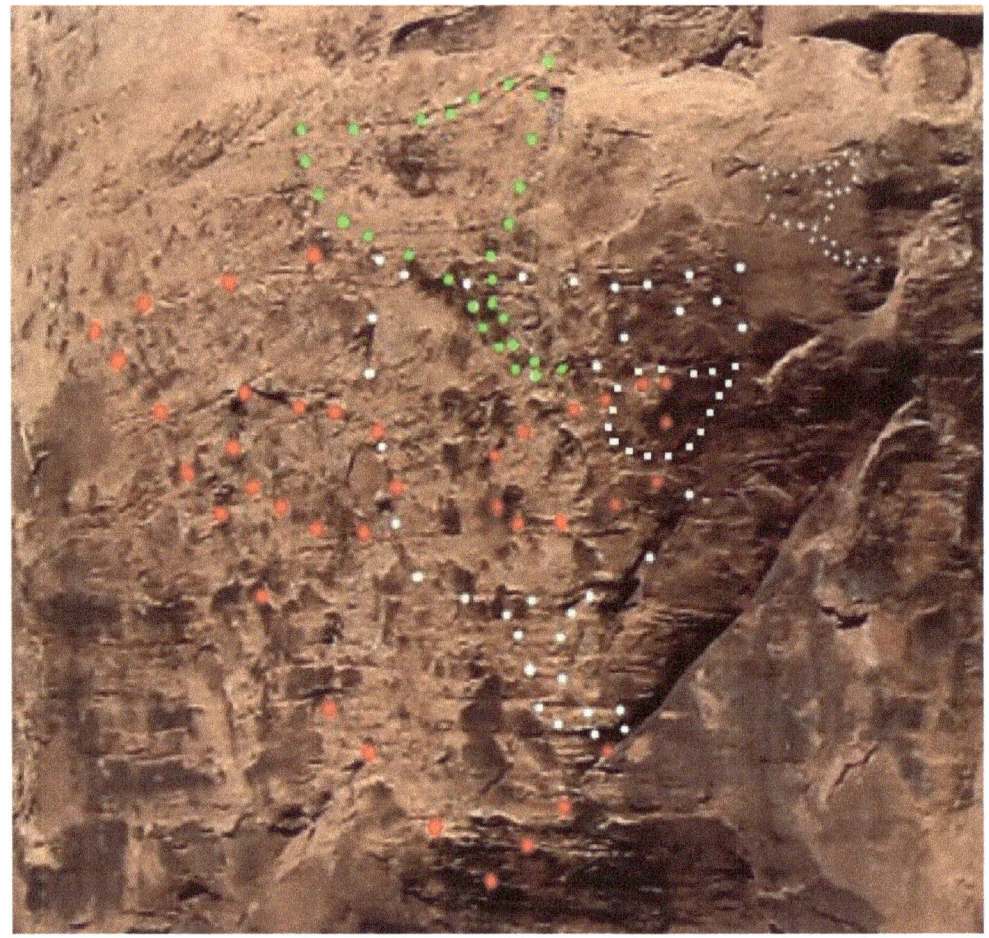

Fig. 4, Close up view of partially traced layered dragon motifs, Arches National Park. Utah USA, from www.wikipedia.org, by author

Hemispheric Comparison of Motifs and Conventions

This section is a categorized gallery of tracings using sculpted heads, caves, inscription rocks, stone tablets and miscellaneous items as examples. The examples presented represent a portion of examples studied that illustrate the Western Hemisphere bird and dragon motifs are stylistically equivalent to their global counterparts. have remained generally unchanged in appearance during the time period covered by my examples, and there are conventions related to their position relative to each other and on an object.

Sculpted Heads

I have included three heads that were personally examined. The first is a 35 pound quartz anthropomorphic head which was found in shallow water of a minor tributary off a river in northern Georgia. More detail is provided on this head because it is in my temporary possession which allowed a closer examination. The second anthropomorphic example is from the Toledo District, Belize and was found in a most unexpected place.

Both were chance finds and were noticed only because of their shape and recognizable eye motif. The third example is an realistic representation of a human head which was found by its owner near Manchester, Kentucky, six feet below the surface during construction excavation. Following these examples will be other heads from Eastern North America followed with examples from other regions of the world.

Georgia USA

One of the universal conventions found on heads is having one or more bird pairs positioned with their beaks meeting at the top of the head. This can be seen in figure 6 where Purple Bird 1 has most of the body showing while bird 2, which is more posterior, has less of the body apparent, with their beaks meeting at the indented area just left of the top of the head. On more realistic heads, the birds serve as hair features on top the head and in some examples are the flowing hair or "side-burns" extending to or beyond the ear.

In most heads reviewed there are more than one bird-pairs meeting at the top. This convention was taken to the extreme on the Georgia head where an unknown number of birds of various sizes meet at both the top and bottom of the head. This is illustrated in figure 7 where prominent pecked eyes have been traced clustered around a partially traced dragon motif.

Fig. 5, Head, Quartzite, 43cm, Georgia, USA, by author

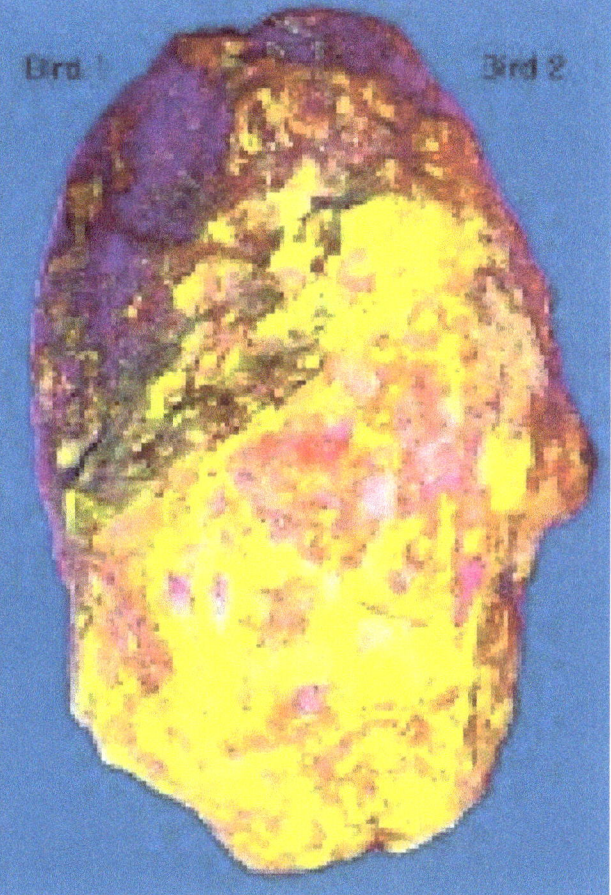

Fig.6, DStretch colorized image showing bird pair with beaks meeting at top of head, by author

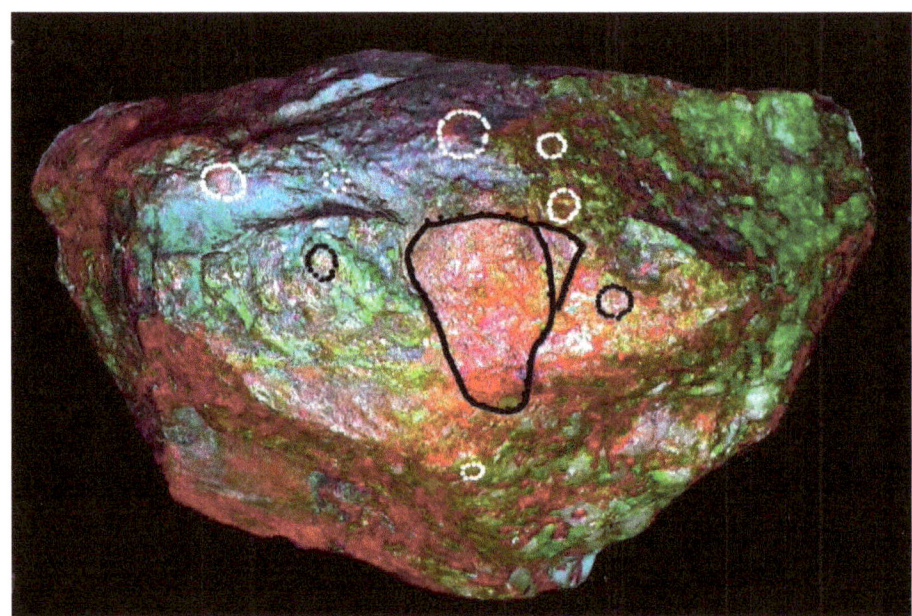

Fig. 7, Top of Georgia head showing bird eyes and partial dragon symbol by author

The partially trace red dragon symbol in figure 7 provides a segue to another convention. Dragon symbols are always present between or near the end of bird beaks or being "grasped" by open parrot beaks. Interestingly, the small area around open beaks often displays as red or another color different than than the adjacent area. This can be seen in the following graphic where three of six larger birds have open beaks around the exceptionally white area on the forehead and on later examples from Kentucky and Belize.

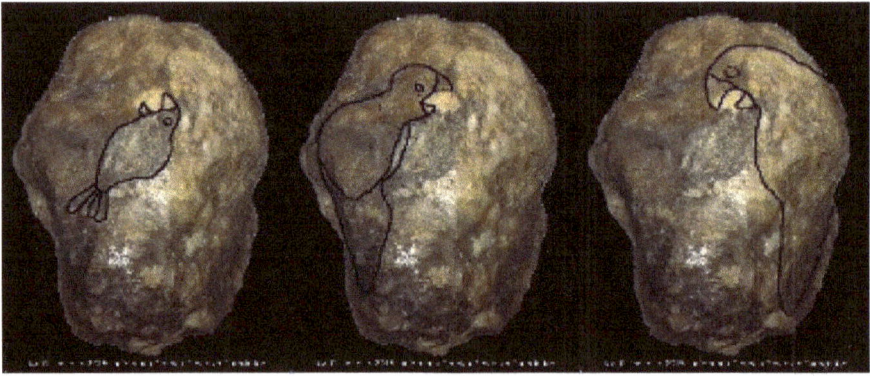

Fig. 8, Three birds "holding" an object, by author

In this example, the dragons are located within the 4 cm white area where there are at least three dragons and three birds (figs. 9, 10) Two dragons are identified by black tracings of their tails and an exquisitely formed eye, and the other by the red face outline. I have only traced two of the birds to avoid cluttering the graphic. One of the unmarked birds is a darker green and is located adjacent to the red bird and the other to the far right of the graphic.

I have not worked with stone, but was intrigued by the small tool marks and especially the contoured shapes forming some of the figures. The dot and dash marks would have required a very small tipped tool, great skill and patience. Since quartz has a Mohs hardness rating of 7, this would exclude the use of metal tools and leaves minerals with a higher rating such as corundum and diamonds. The micro-tooling can be seen in figure 10 where circular features are noted along with the tail of the black dragon face in the upper left corner.

With respect to the bas-relief shapes, it is not unreasonable to assume the artist took advantage of naturally formed multi-dimensional features that would resemble bird and dragon outlines to work with. However, I get the impression some would have required human modifications. This is a speculative observation and it is hoped the head can be examined by a specialist in a laboratory setting.

An unanswered question is why this small area has remained white, while the balance of the rock has been discolored by minerals from the flowing water.

Fig. 9, birds and dragons in 4 cm area of Georgia head, by author

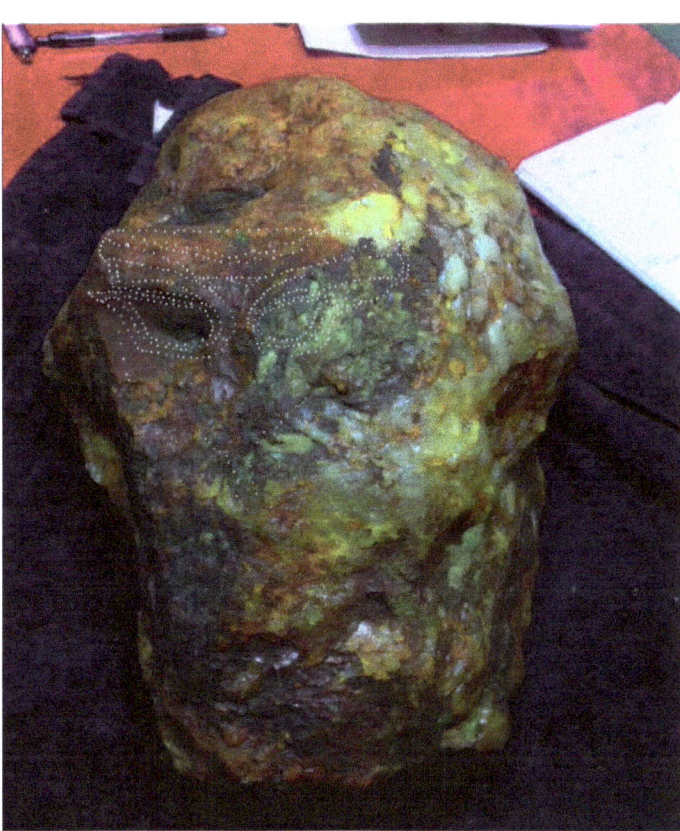

Fig.11, Partial tracing of complex dragon symbol, by author

Figure 10, Magnified view of upper right quadrant of figure 9 showing tool marks, by author

Toledo District, Belize

This head follows the convention of multiple birds converging at both ends of heads, inscription tablets and other objects. Dragon symbols are located at the both ends where the beaks converge and these small areas produce a different color when viewed with image enhancement software (figure 13). The blue area in the white birds beak has been outlined for emphasis.

The picture orientation in figure 13 has been rotated to properly orient three larger dragon depictions diagonally spanning the lower half of the head. The largest can be located by its crimson pear shaped nose, which has a small orange dragon on the end. Adjacent and to the right of the crimson nose, is the pale green nose of another face and there are two more smaller dragons to it's right. One should be able to visualize some of the upward slanting almond shaped eye features.

This head was a serendipitous find under a tree in a Southern Belize town and captured my attention because of its shape and two prominent dragon eyes. Because it is a semi-secluded location, it has unceremoniously become a target for men when nature calls. This and the 80 plus degree temperature limited close examination to how long I could hold my breath. A significant number of motifs were observed in some of the most unexpected locations, such as decorative rocks in flower beds and the large limestone blocks at Fort George park in Belize City. I have included examples from Barnes Cave near San Ignacio in the Cave Section.

Fig. 12 Grotesque head with motifs, Toledo District, Belize CA, by author

Fig. 13, Birds holding object, by author

Manchester, Kentucky, USA

This example provided very prominent tool marks to trace two dragon motifs. The dragon eye cartouches and eye-brows were surprisingly uncluttered with other images permitting accurate tracing. The orientation of the dragon faces on both sides of this head is unique. On heads, the dragon face and tail have the same general orientation as the head. On rocks and escarpments it has a north-south orientation with the tail heading towards the ground. Because of this convention and since the back of the head is flat, it is reasonable to assume the artist's intent was for it to be displayed in a prone position.

The enhanced images indicate possible red pigment residue on the forehead area (figure 16) and on the small area between the beaks of two birds (figure 15).

Fig 14, Sculpted head, Manchester, KY USA, photo by owner, modified by author

Fig. 15. Sculpted head, birds holding an object, Manchester, KY USA, by author

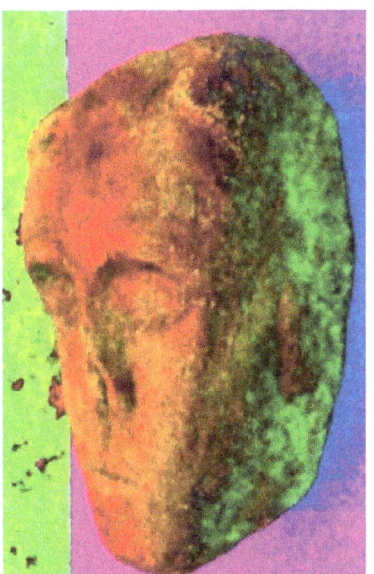

Fig. 16, Sculpted head, showing dark red dot on forehead,, by author

Southern Ohio USA
This example obtained from the internet is believed to be from Southern Ohio, but could not be confirmed with the owner or other sources. This head is one of a number of artifacts from the Ohio River Valley region analyzed that display the two motifs.

Fig.17, Head, various views, possibly Southern Ohio, USA, from internet source, modifications by author

Michigan Lower Peninsula, USA
Pictures for this example were furnished by the owner who received it as a gift twenty five years ago. The only information supplied was that it was found in a woods in southern Michigan.

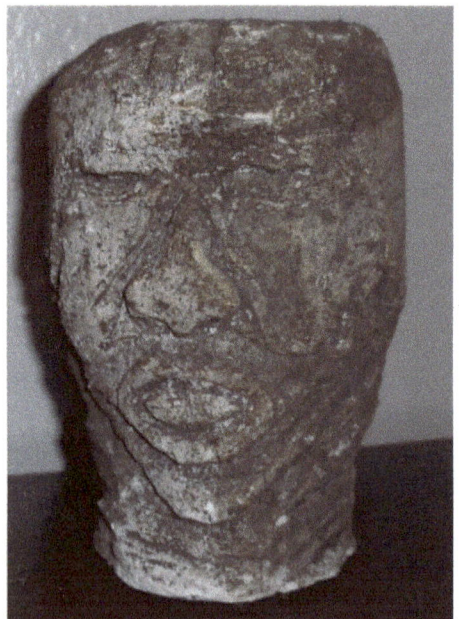 

Fig. 18, Head, Southern Michigan USA, from owner

Fig. 19, Side view with motifs, from owner, modifications by author

Illinois or Missouri USA

This example exemplifies the level of detail that can be achieved on a small figure. It was bought and resold several years ago by a antiquity dealer in central Illinois who only recalls it was purchased in Illinois or Missouri. Measuring only 1 5/8 inches in height, this mustached grandfatherly looking man has multiple bird pairs and dragon faces. Interestingly, one of the dragon face motifs on his chin (not traced) gives the impression of a goatee.

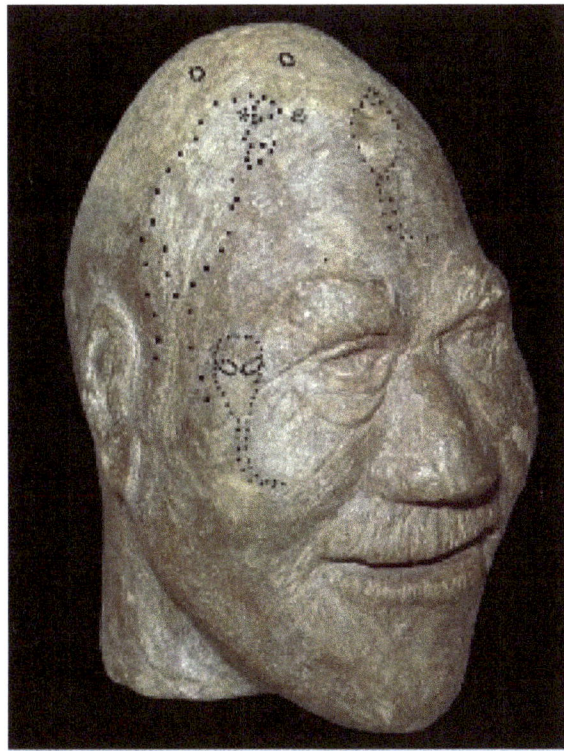

Fig. 20, Miniature head, Illinois or Missouri USA, www.americasprideantiques.com, Modifications by author

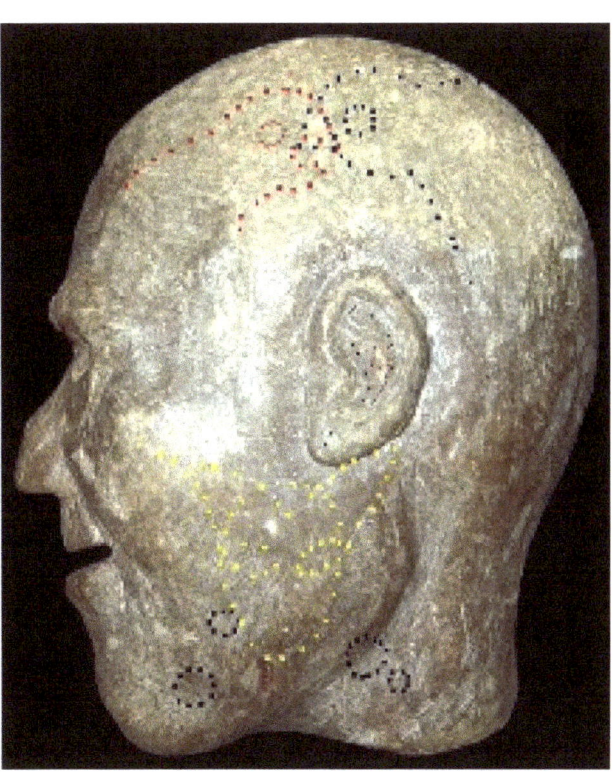

Fig. 21, Bird pair, dragon, traced eyes.

The detail on this diminutive head can be seen in the bird depictions in the ear. Please note the red tracing of a dragon face, incorporated in the body of the larger bird such as seen in figure 19 and other examples.

The tool marks forming the black eye and unmarked beak on the ear lobe was quite obvious when viewed on a computer monitor. It appears to me, the outline of the balance of the ear is filled with bird head pairs, a convention noted in other examples, however the picture resolution limited certainty.

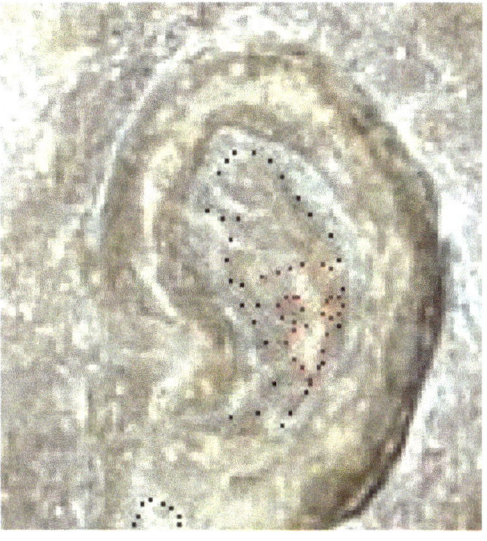

Fig. 22, Ear with miniature figures, by Author.

Global Examples

Easter Island

Software analysis of Moai heads from Easter Island proved to be difficult but not impossible. It is believed this was a result of the porous surface of the rock or perhaps lack of pigment or weathering. However there was sufficient tool marks and color indications permitting tracing several birds with some confidence.

As with other examples, there are multiple eye features clustered to gather indicating the presence of a bird heads, but defining the heads was impossible.

Because I could not locate a picture showing the top area of the head, confirming the convention of birds coming up the side of the head with beaks meeting at the top was not possible. It does appear that the elongated hair features on all the heads could stylistically represent the lower portion of the body and tail feathers, with the balance of the bird located on the forehead area.

As usual, the dragon images were identifiable because of eye shapes and also showed evidence of being stacked on top each other. The elongated double-line eye-brow was particularly noticeable as shown in figure 24.

Figure 23, Moai Head, approx.1-1,000 CE, modified by author, from https://wheresmike.wordpress.com/

Fig.24, Moai Head, Easter Island, from http://galleryhip.com/easter-island-heads.html, by author

Fig. 25, Eye inlay of Moai statue, from www.scottedelman.com/, by author

The use of small imagery as was seen on the earlier Georgia head example, continues on the Moai heads on the only inlayed eye artifact ever found. In high resolution digital format, the level of detail is striking. There are multiple birds on the eye and on the periphery of the eye socket. The dragon face on the pupil was particularly noticeable in the digital format.

Turkey
Nemrut Dagi in south-east Turkey is the location of the House of the Gods and temple-tomb of King Antiochus I (69-34 BCE). The picture montage in figure 26 was chosen because it produced, though marginally, color variations, location of eyes and tooling aiding in the interpretation and tracing of some motifs. The center and left heads are filled with many fairly discernible motifs however they could not be traced with any certainty.

I could not locate a stone head of Antiochus I, but a coin with his likeness surprisingly displays both motifs (Fig. 27). I have noted a bird pair at the top of his head with red dots and one on the ear lobe in green. Even the poor fellow's nose was transformed into a birds head. A close view of the ends of many of his hair locks have a feature I would interpret as an eye which produces a bird head appearance.

Fig. 26, Nemrut-Dagi, turkey, modified from www.romeartlover.tripod.com by author

Fig.27, Antiochus I gold stater, 275 BCE, from wikipedia.org, by author

From a similar time period at nearby at Antiochia ad Cragum, this example is a Roman or Greek influenced head of Aphrodite discovered in 2013 by the University of Nebraska-Lincoln archaeology team. In this example, the artist has used the head's left eye as the head of the bird located on the left cheek and extending to the chin (untraced). This is convention was observed in other examples.

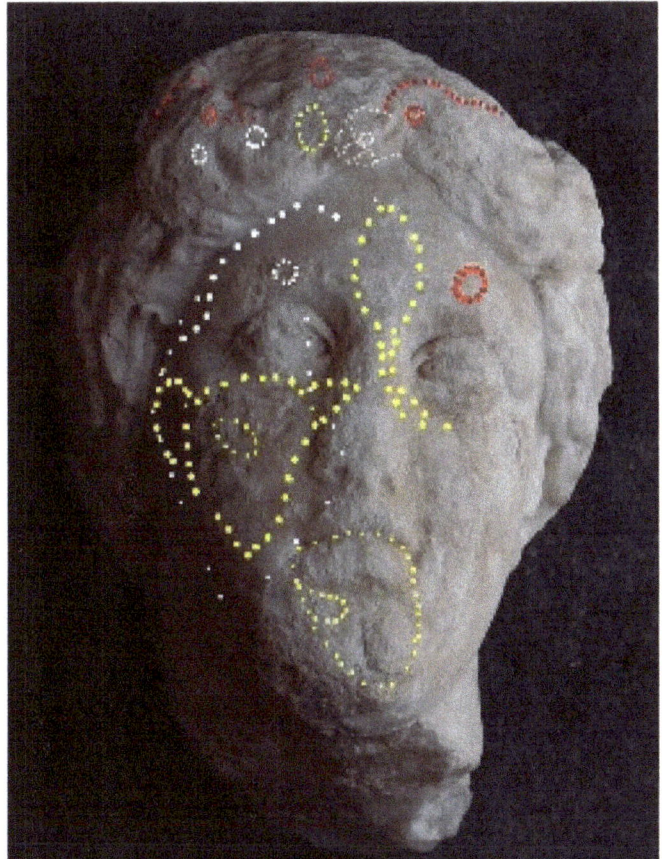

Figure 28, Aphrodite, Turkey c. 50 CE or later, modified from www.heritagedaily.com

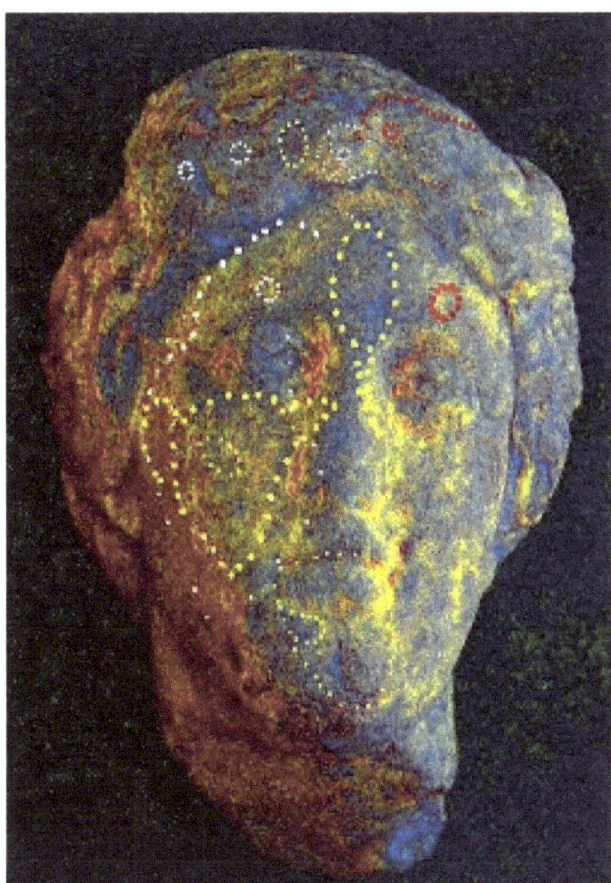

Fig. 29 Aphrodite, Turkey, c. 50 CE or later, enhanced image. modified from www.heritagedaily.com

The Indus Valley
The examples from Mohenjo-daro clearly showed the use of the two motifs (figs. 30 & 31), however the image quality of figure 30 prohibited close scrutiny of the head band, but it gives the impression of two bird heads meeting. In figure 31, the bird pair is more evident in the hair area above and to the right of the headband center piece. Both examples from this region are dated 2600 BCE which pushes the timeline back considerably.

Figure 32 illustrates the lingering question of when some of the motifs were applied. In many cases, the placement of the motifs give the impression they were graffiti added later in time. In this example, the rough texture of the dragon face on the chest disrupts the pattern of the clothing creating the impression it may have been added later.

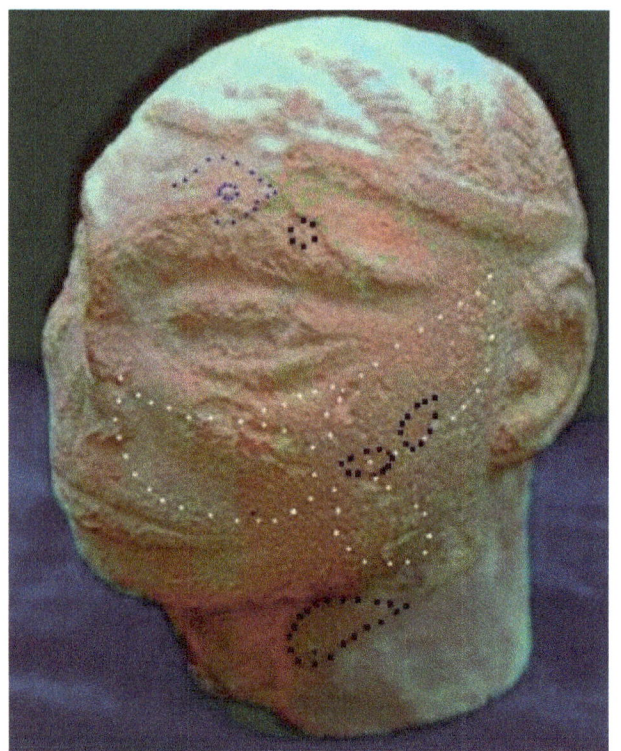

Fig. 30, Terracotta head Mohenjo-daro, Pakistan ,2600 BCE, modified from http://realhistoryww.com

Figure 31, Sculpted Head from Mohenjo-daro, Pakistan, ca. 2600BCE, modified from www.sjsu.edu

Fig. 32, Torso view of figure 31, by author from internet source

British Isles

The following five examples indicate the motifs were in use in the British Isles sometime during the Medieval Period (400-1500 CE)

Figs. 33, 34, Late medieval sculpted head, Corinium Museum, from commons.wikipedia.org

Fig. 35. Janus figure, Boa Island, Scotland, by author

Fig, 36, Two layered opposing bird heads, Boa Island, Scotland, by author

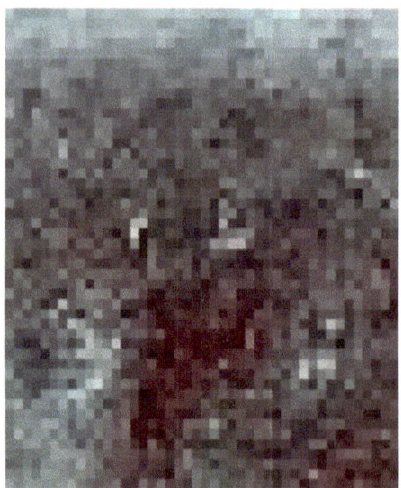

Fig. 37, Magnified small dragon outline on forehead showing dash and dot tool marks

Peru

The sculpted heads below were discovered at Chavin de Huantar in Huaraz, Peru in 2013 by Dr. John Rick of Stanford University and are dated to 1500 BCE. The locks of hair are bird shaped with eyes.

The head in figure 39 is particularly telling with it's volute shaped fang and "goggle eyes", both of which are diagnostic elements in depictions of the Mayan rain god Chac, and Tlaloc, the name used by the later 14th century Aztec (figures 40 & 41).

Fig. 38, Sculpted head, Chavin de Huantar in Huaraz, Peru, 1500 BCE, photo by Dr. John Rick, modifications by author

Fig. 39, Sculpted head, Chavin de Huantar in Huaraz, Peru, 1500 BCE, photo by Dr. John Rick, modifications by author

Fig.40, Mayan Chaac, from wikipedia.org

Fig. 41, Aztec Tlaloc, from flicker.com, by author

Mexico

Fig. 42, Chaac head dress, with some bird and dragon motifs, by author

Fig. 43, Chaac shield with partially traced birds, untraced dragon motif on center area, by author

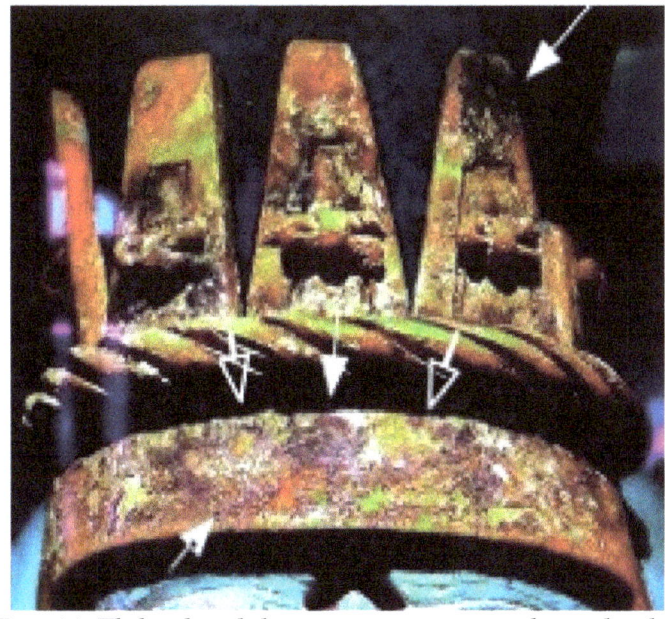

Fig. 44, Tlaloc head dress, open arrows indicate bird, closed arrows indicates dragon, by author

The color stretched images of Chaac produced red areas filling the outline of several birds that did not show in the original photograph. The Tlaloc head dress produced separate colors aiding identification of images. The two birds facing the dragon motif was particularly evident. It is interesting to see the shield displayed displayed two colors. It is not known if this was the result of pigments or created as a result of a shadow produced by illumination.

Fig. 45, Olmec head from unknown site, select paired bird and dragons, from www.glogster.com, modifications by author

Fig. 46, Olmec head, close up of right eye, right "horn" not traced, by author

The stone step pictured below is located at the extreme right of the first row of steps facing Plaza V at the Mayan ruin of Labaantun, Belize. It's dark color with the tan center made it very noticeable compared with the balance of the steps which were lighter in color. I have no explanation for the dark color but have observed it on other examples. I found another rock with the motifs in a pile of rubble adjacent to the plaza. If visiting the site, look into the creek on your right as you cross on the path leading to the interpretative center.

Figs. 47, Stone step, Labaantun, Belize CA, by author

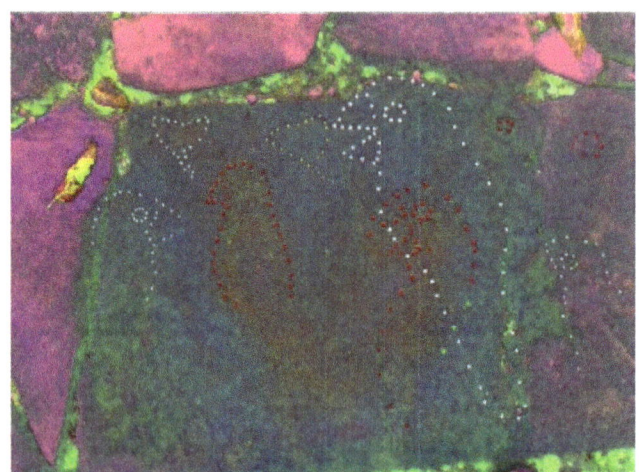

Fig. 48, Color stretched image with bird and dragon motifs, Labaatun, BZ, by author

Fig. 49, Yaxha stelae depicting Mesoamerican rain god, from Wikipedia Commons

Fig. 50, Yaxha stelae, viewers lower right, by author

Caves

In this venue both motifs are positioned over and around the cave entrance with others appearing on adjacent escarpments. On escarpments, birds are many times positioned facing naturally formed fissures and holes which in Chinese mythology represents the womb of the earth[2]. This convention was particularly noticeable on the escarpment along the creek leading to the Barnes Cave entrance shown in a later example.

Cave-in Rock, Southern Illinois, USA, on the Ohio River

The once colorful escarpment and massive entrance must have been an impressive site for the ancient traveller on the Ohio River. The ceiling is a tapestry of images featuring a large set of dragon eyes just inside the entrance. Tool marks on the escarpment can be seen with the unassisted eye.

Fig. 51, Two bird-pairs, large bird and dragon eye, Cave-in Rock, by author

Fig.52, Ceiling, bird-pairs, red dragon face, arrows point to other dragon face outlines, Cave-in-Rock, by author

---

[2] Dr. Siu-Lueng Lee, personal conversation

Fig. 53, Ceiling Cave-in-Rock with partially traced dragon and birds, by author

Barnes Cave, San Ignacio, BZ CA

Fig. 54, Entrance to Barnes Cave, BZ CA, by author

Fig. 55, Entrance, Large parrot head (not traced) with partial dragons, Barnes Cave, BZ CA, by author

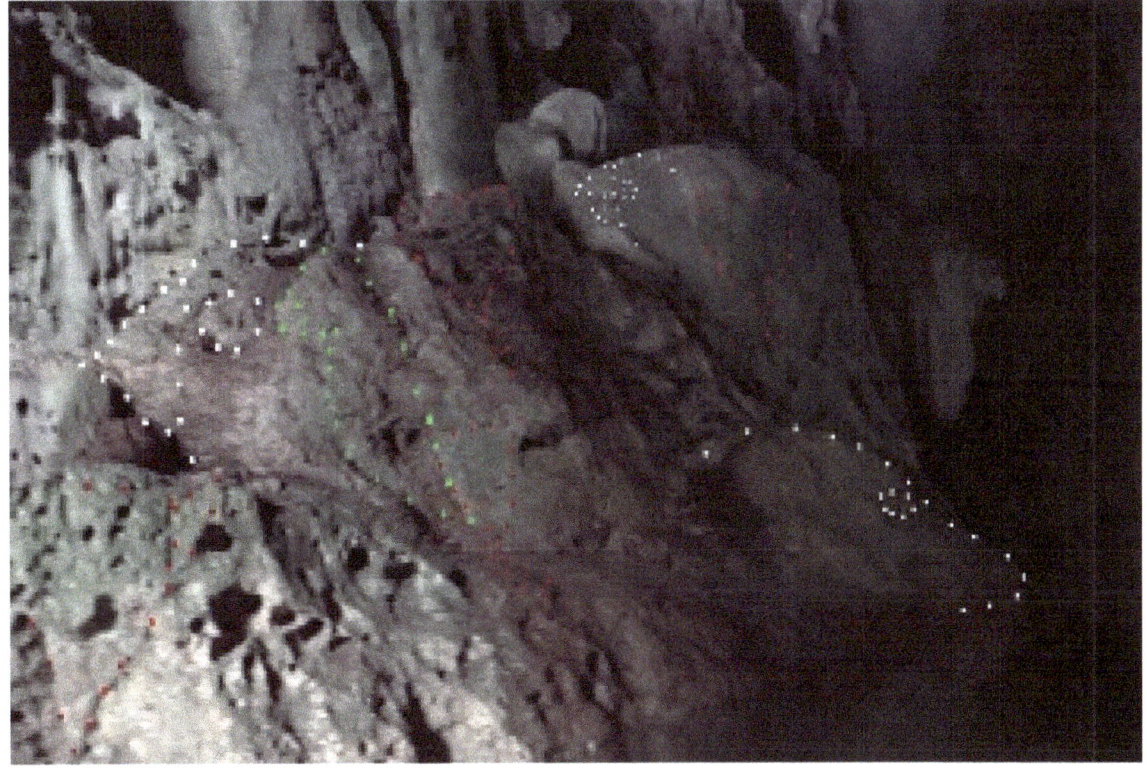

Fig. 56, Natural color image birds and dragons, Barnes Cave, BZ CA, by author

Barnes cave has a prolific amount of both motifs of various sizes on the escarpment along the creek leading to the cave and around the small lagoon at the cave entrance. Tool marks on the larger figures were large and obvious, making the forms recognizable almost at first glance, however vegetation was somewhat problematic. Some of the larger forms are traced in the preceding photographs. The interior of the cave was filled with natural features resembling bird heads, some of which were quite dramatic looking. The dragon motif also appeared in significant quantity on the walls along the water permitting close examination and they also appear at higher elevations in the cave. Those near the water had their tails extending to the water line.

On a relatively horizontal area approximately 150 feet into the cave, is a faded red feature which at first glance gives the impression a large parrot, perhaps 10 feet long. The head traced in white is to the viewers left. For unknown reason ,the color is different than the adjacent rock and creates a very dramatic and identifiable bird form. (Figure 56) Subsequent tracings showed additional birds and dragons placed on the larger bird.

Cuevas de las Maravillas, La Romana, Dominican Republic
As with the previous examples, this large and impressive cave had numerous motifs which could be easily recognized. At several locations withing the cave there were clusters of rock art (figure 58) which according to museum explanations represent drawings of the Taino culture who migrated to Caribbean region from South America. Because of diseases carried by 16th century Spanish, they became extinct, thus the Taino drawings would presumably have occurred prior to that time.

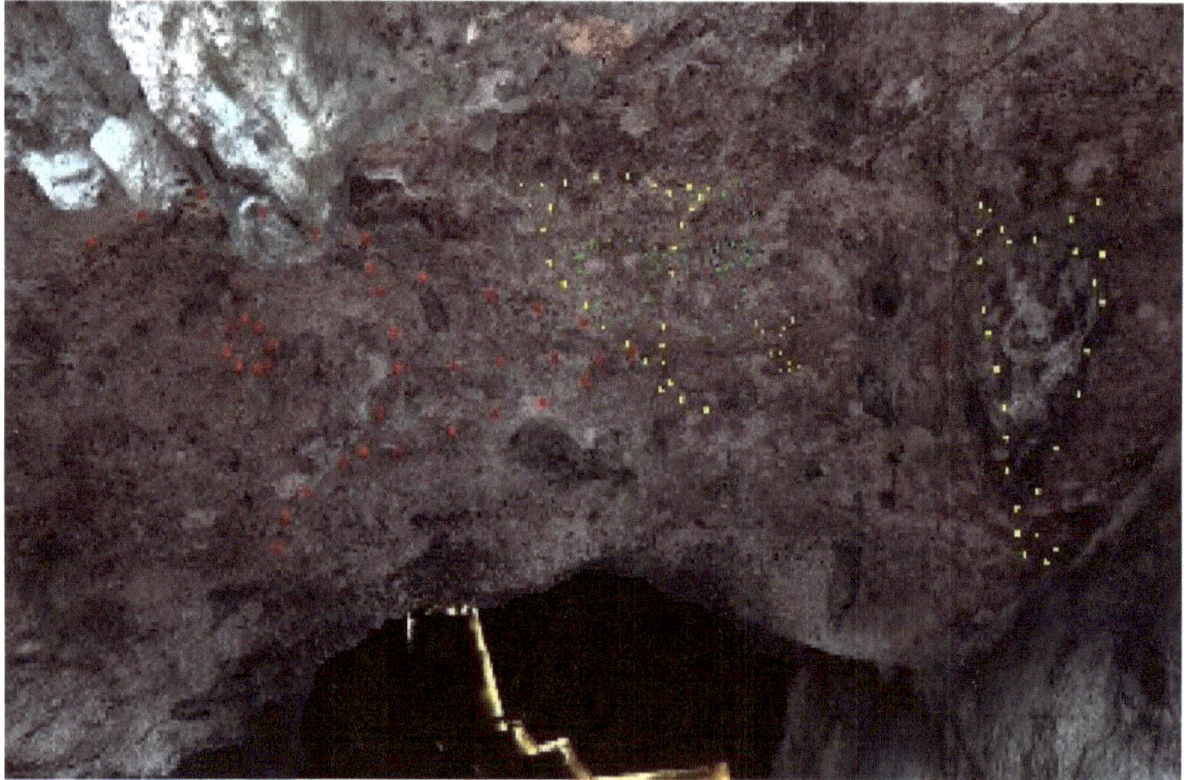

Fig. 57, Multiple bird-pairs and dragons, situated around main entrance, Cuevas de las Maravillas, Dominican Repubulic, by author

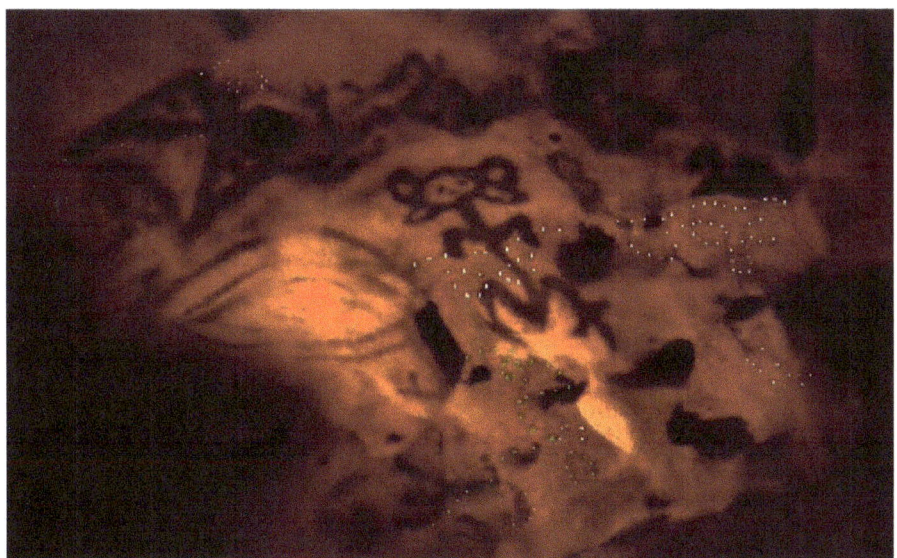

Fig. 58, Birds and dragons and Taino art, Cuevas de las Maravillas, Dominican Republic, by author

The magnified Taino symbol in figure 59 is noteworthy because of it's stylistic similarity to the bird-pair of the Chinese P'eng symbols (figures 60, 61) located in the North American Southwest region. The P'eng symbol, is one of the earliest Chinese script symbols indicating 'friendship' and is depicted as two birds 'joined at the breast'[3].

In both examples there is evidence indicating the more prominent stylistic bird pairs were placed over the earlier more realistic appearing bird-pairs. In figure 59 a discernible beak outline, noted in green, leads to the black oval shape indicating the location of an obscured head. Likewise in the New Mexico example, I have traced a realistic bird-pair whose body contours coincide with the later pictogram. On the surface, this suggests both symbols may have a related meaning and only separated by time.

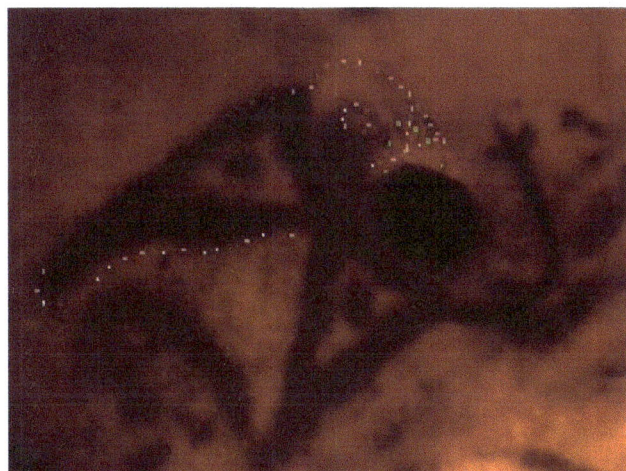

Fig. 59, Taino symbol close up, Cuevas de las Maravillas, Dominican Republic, by author

Fig. 60, P'eng symbol, from Dr. John Ruskamp, Jr., by author

---

[3] Dr. John A. Ruskamp, Jr, *Asiatic Echos*, page 68

Fig. 61, Partial tracings, Boca Negra Canyon, Petroglyph National Monument, New Mexico USA, by author

Mellissani Cave, Greece.

Fig. 62, Birds and dragons, Melissani Cave, Greece, from www.canuckabroad.com, by author

Fig. 63, Close view birds and dragons, from www.canuckabroad.com, by author

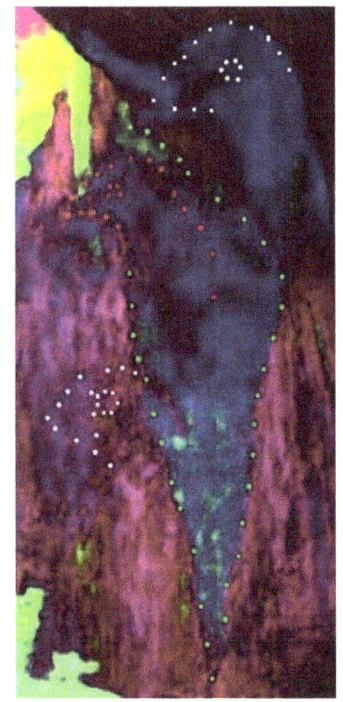

Fig. 64, Birds, close view, by author

Fig. 65, Melissani Cave, from www.canuckabroad.com,

Arches National Park, Utah USA
Though not a cave, but because of the similarity with the previous example, I could not resist including this North American landmark.

Fig. 66, Larger birds and two dragons, Arches National Park, Utah USA, from www.wikipedia.org, by author

The outline of the smaller white bird was quite easy to determine because of prominent tool marks and aided by it's form displayed in different red color than the surrounding area (figure 66). With at least three heads converging at the large white bird head, identifying which beak went with what head was difficult. As a result, I believe the lower beak of the large white bird belongs to another bird. The beak-in beak motif is particularly evident on the arch along with another convention of conflating the dragon face and beak (figure 67)

There are a number of dragons scattered around the rock but concentrated in the area shown in figure 68. The convention of layering this symbol is illustrated with the overlapping of the left red eye with a smaller white eye. The circular feature in the upper right corner of figure 66 is very exacting and has tool marks around the perimeter. I could not determine if it is an element of a larger figure or a stand alone feature. Regardless it is an example of the significant amount of artistic work performed on this monolith.

Fig. 67, Beak-in-beak motif, various dragon faces, Arches National Park, Utah USA, from www.wikipedia.org, by author

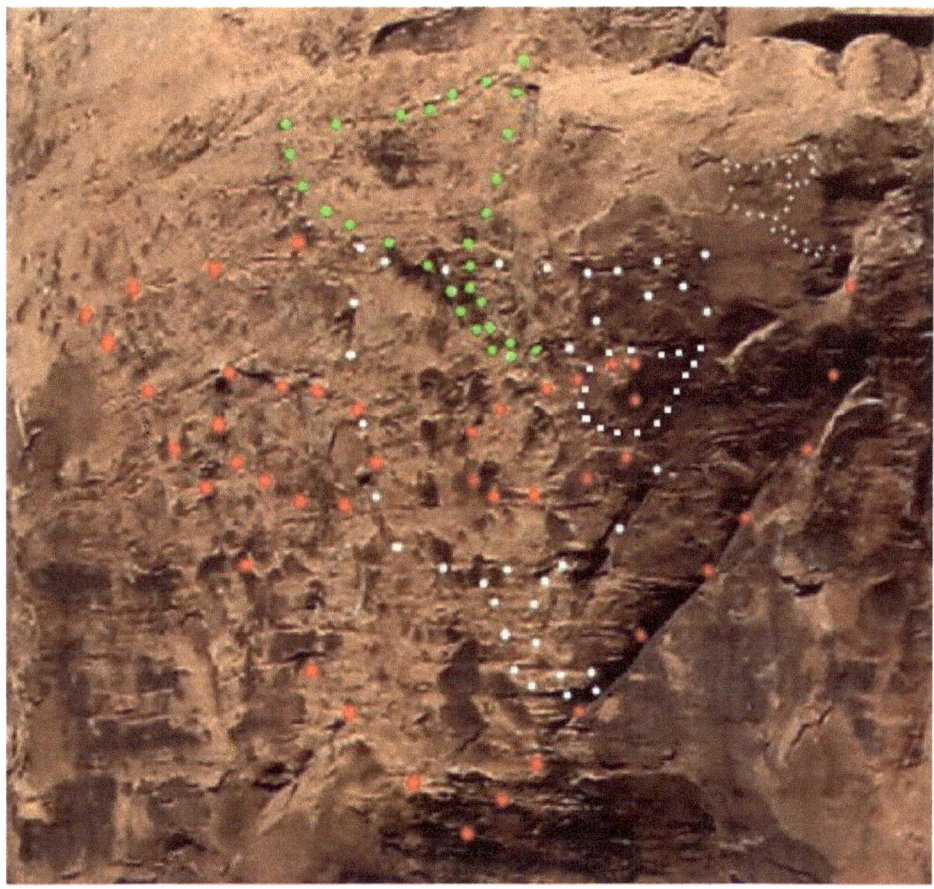

Fig. 68, Partially traced dragon motifs, Arches National Park, by author

Old Man's Cave & Upper Water Fall, Ohio, USA

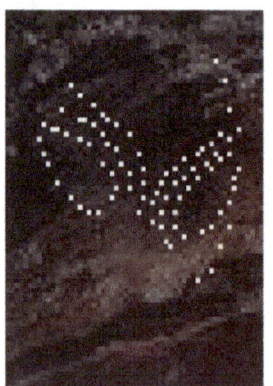

Fig. 69, Old Man's Cave, southeastern Ohio, from www.backcountrygallery.com, modified by author

Fig. 70, Upper Falls, Hocking Hills southeastern Ohio, from www.backcountrygallery.com, modified by author with two close view inserts.

Inscription Rocks and Tablets

Judaculla Inscription Rock, North Carolina, USA

Despite the numerous pock marks, tool marks and color forms were discernible permitting fairly accurate tracings. The lower third of the rock, which was exposed by a professional archeologist in 2008, aided in identifying two dragon symbols with head dresses. There are approximately seven small rocks between the large rock and the access road that are free of the clutter of the large rock and display the two motifs clearly (figure 72).

Fig. 71, Judaculla Rock, North Carolina showing bird and dragon motifs, by author

Fig. 72, Small rock at Judaculla, by author

Inscription Rock, Kelleys Island, Ohio USA
Pictures suitable for analysis limited the amount of images that could be traced with certainty, however the two tracings shown were quite obvious. There are suggestions of several birds and dragons clustered in the immediate area of the tracings, but could not be traced well.

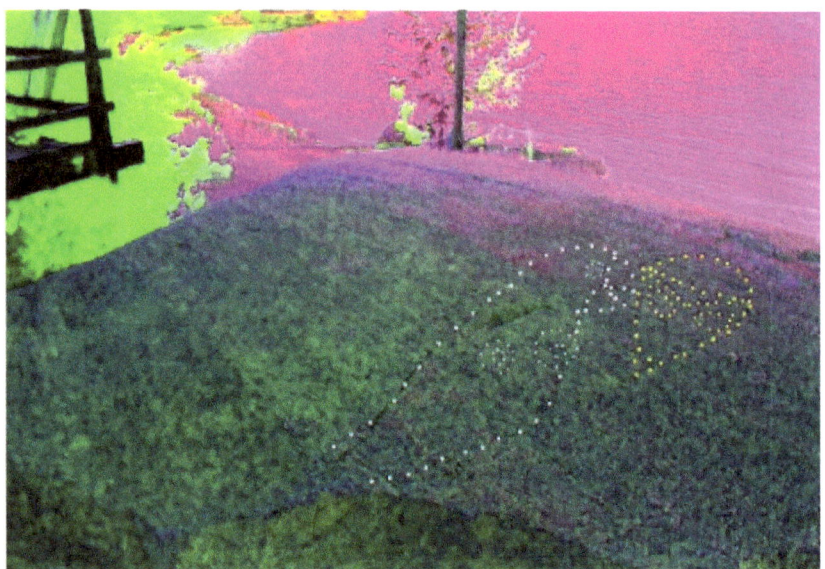

Fig. 73, Inscription Rock, Kelleys Island, Ohio, from www.collegegreenmag.com, modified by author

Tablets
Sumerian (Iraq and Kuwait) Tablet

Fig. 74, Sumerian cuneiform tablet, 16th-15th century BCE, from www.metmuseum.org, by author

The tablets in figures 74 and 75 were challenging to work with, but some features were discernible to permit tracing. The script in both examples appear to have been applied later suggesting perhaps the tablets were "re-cycled." Please note the division of color in the color stretched image of the Jehoash tablet which may indicate pigment residue.

Israel Jehoash Tablet

Fig. 75, Jehoash Tablet, approximate 800 BCE, from www.timesofisrael.com

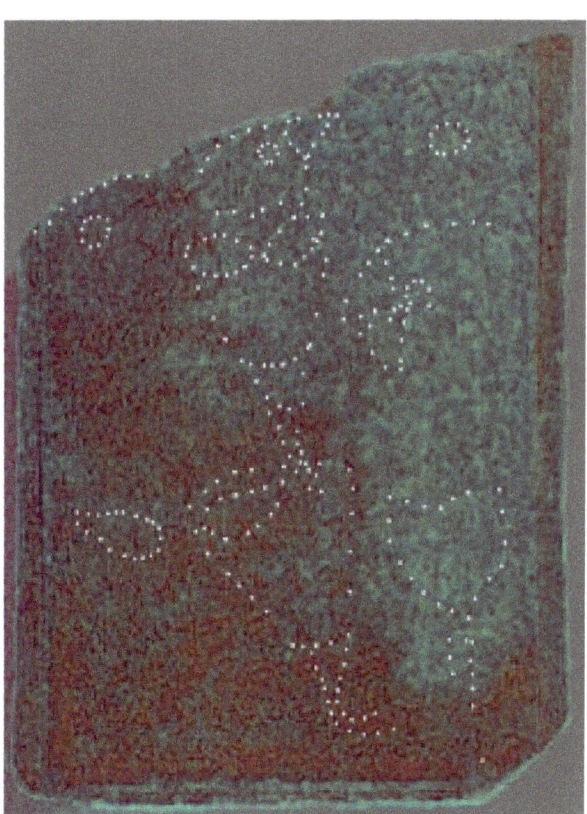
Fig. 76, Jehoash Tablet showing bird and dragon motifs, bi-color division, from www.timesofisrael.com, by author

Ohio, USA

These unique North American examples (figures 77 & 78) are two of approximately 50 tablets and three obelisks discovered in early 2015. Though some have been disturbed presumably by a logging road cut thru the site, they appear to have been standing upright originally and aligned in rows.

Three styles have been observed to date: cartouche with raised center area, cartouche with depressed center area, and no cartouche. The framework consists of a series of small bird-heads facing each other.

The bird and dragon motifs appear on the tablets and obelisks reviewed to date. Some of those reviewed, show signs of pigment residue which were amplified when viewed with color stretching software.

The convention of layering and stacking bird heads can be seen in figure 75. In the lower right corner a white parrot head shares space with long beak head. The top of another head passes thru the bottom of the black eye and has an untraced eye visible.

There are a minimum of three more heads in the purple area above the traced heads. An eye of an unmarked bird is visible in the upper left corner.

Fig. 77A, Partial dragon tracings, by author

Fig. 77, Ohio tablet with partial bird pair and dragon motifs, by author

Fig. 78, Ohio tablet with bird-pair and dragon motifs, by author

Favorite Examples

Georgia USA

This is an exacting and well executed figurine found within ten feet of the Chinese sword. Please note the perfect circular untraced bird eyes on the shoulders and tiny birds on the feathers of the head dress. The level of detail of the computer screen could not be duplicated in this format.

Fig. 79, 14cm figurine with dragon, birds and untraced birds on shoulders, Georgia USA, by author

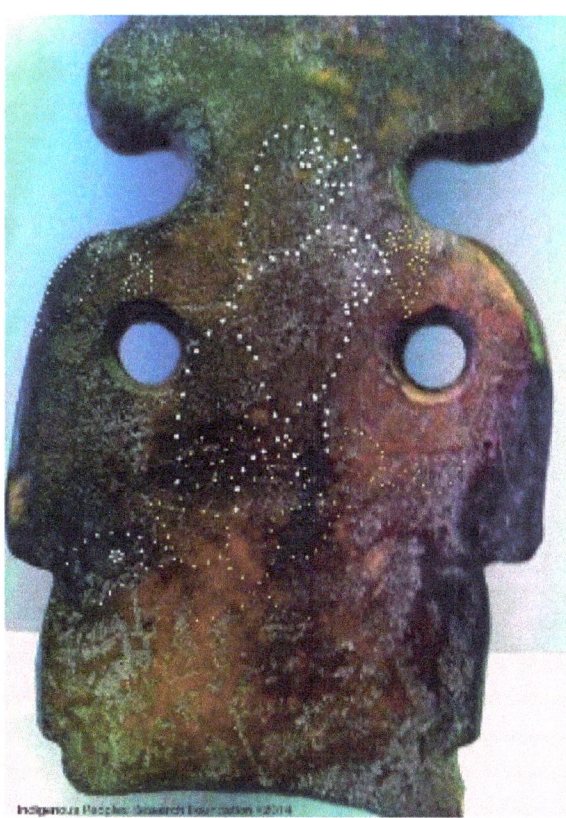

Fig. 80, 14cm figurine reverse, by author

Fig. 79a, Close up of birds on head dress feathers, by author

Ethiopia Church of St. George

This example is one of eleven churches at Lalibela carved in rock during the 13th century and is named after St. George the Dragon Slayer.

Fig. 81, St. George's church, aerial view, photo by George Steinmetz, by author

Fig. 82, Church of St. George, with select bird and dragon motifs, by author

China Examples in Chronological Order

The earliest bird shaped examples from China found in this research are from the Paleolithic Laonainaimiao site in Henan Province. Multiple bird outlines were fairly discernible and showed typical layout of stacking birds of various sizes vertically. The bodies of at least two birds on figure 83 were obscured by identification script. There are more figures on these two examples but they could not be traced with any accuracy.

Fig. 83, Paleolithic Bird shape, Laonainaimiao, Henan Province China, from www.kaogu.cn, by author

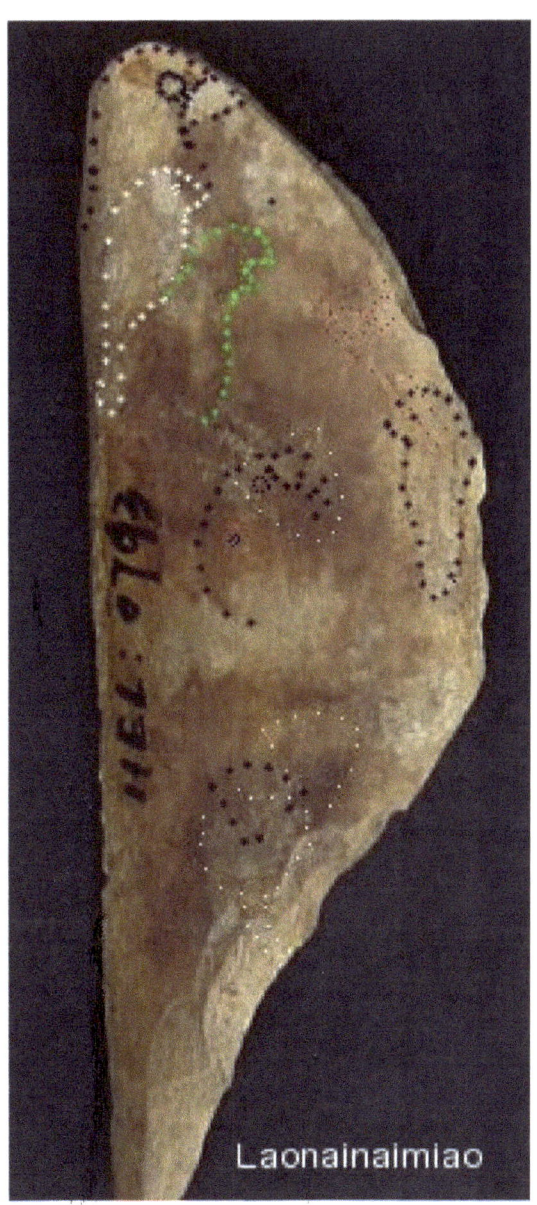

Fig. 84, Paleolithic Bird shape, Laonainaimiao, Henan Province China, from www.kaogu.cn, by author

This example is a Late Paleolithic artifact from Shuidonggou site in northwest China. Like all photographs of Paleolithic artifacts available thru internet sources, it lacks resolution, however in this example the dragon-faces were traced with more confidence. Two elements of the dragon motif that I use for conformation are the tail and at least one eye positioned correctly within the face outline.

Fig. 85, Two tracings of an Engraved Paleolithic artifact, Shuidonggou, China, from www.heritagedaily.com, by author

The motifs become more defined on painted pottery during the Neolithic Period (10,000-2,000 BCE approximate). It was also the period when artistic traditions were expressed on jade objects. For practical purposes of comparison, the stylization of the motifs from this period do not differ from later time periods.

Fig 86, Peiligang Culture pottery 6,000-5200 BCE, Shanghai Museum, color stretched image with partial bird, bird eyes and dragon outlines, wikipedia.org, color modified by author

Fig. 87, Dadiwan Culture Gansu, 5800-3000 BCE, color stretched image with partial bird and dragon outlines and eyes, from http://www.gansumuseum.com, color modified by author

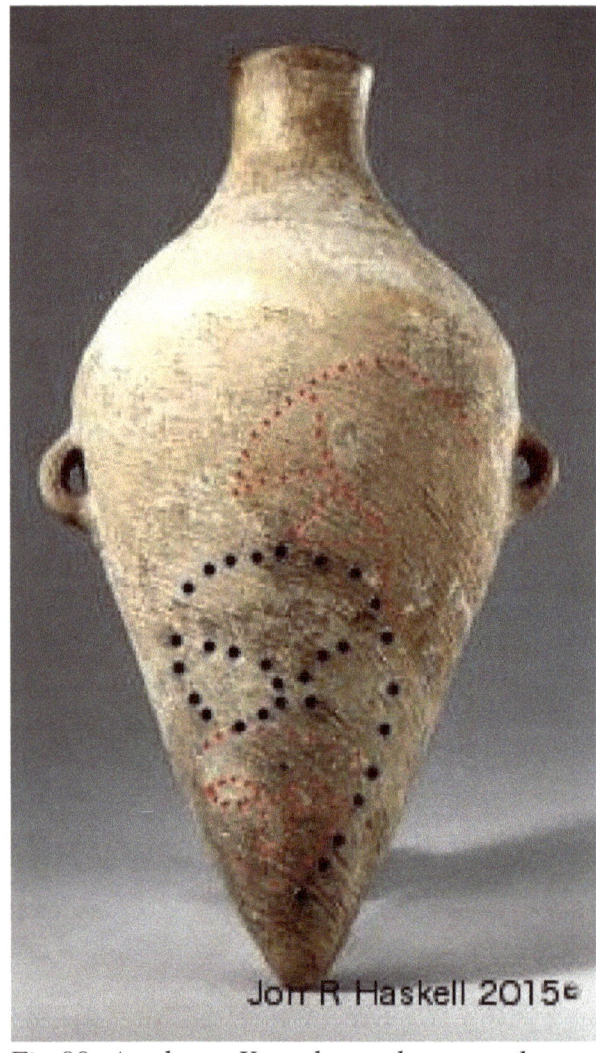

Fig 88, Amphora, Yangshao culture, southern Shaanxi Province, Banpo type, 4800-3600 BCE, www.christies.com , by author

Fig. 89, Color stretched image, Yangshao cord marked amphora, Banpo phase, 4800 BCE, Shaanxi, from wikipedia.org, by author

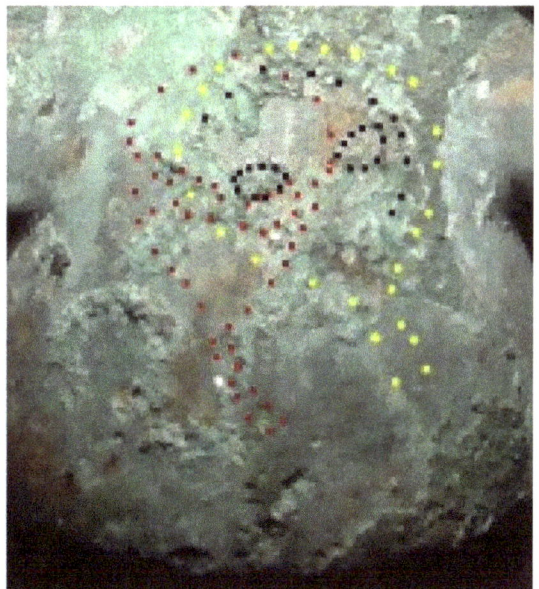

Fig. 91, Close view of nose of Sanxingdui figure showing partial dragon motifs, by author

Fig. 90, Bronze Figure, Sanxingdui 1750-1150 BCE, birds and dragons,from http://www.civilization.org.uk, by author

The silk painting in the following graphic is particularly telling. First, very faint bird and dragon figures appear "behind" more prominent art . This was also noted in a later Song Dynasty painting (figure 94).

Also, there are two different depictions of the dragon on the same canvas. Left center is the head of a long serpentine dragon version that flows to the opposite side of the canvas, and in the center is the faint outline of another dragon face with the distinctive pointed eye. And last, the serpentine dragon form is stylistically equivalent to one appearing on an Ohio Adena artifact which is shown in the following North American section.

A possible explanation for painting over previous art is merely to reuse the canvas which is a practice that continues today. But another reason maybe associated with the changes overtime on how the dragon was depicted It is possible the older version fell in disfavor. An analogy may be the fate of exquisite Sanxingdui artifacts (figure 90) that were broken, burned and carefully buried in 1200 BCE.

It is suggested that this was a "decommissioning" act of sacred objects.

The artist outlined the large dragon-face with painted dots which made tracing very easy with the exception of one eye (Figure 93)

 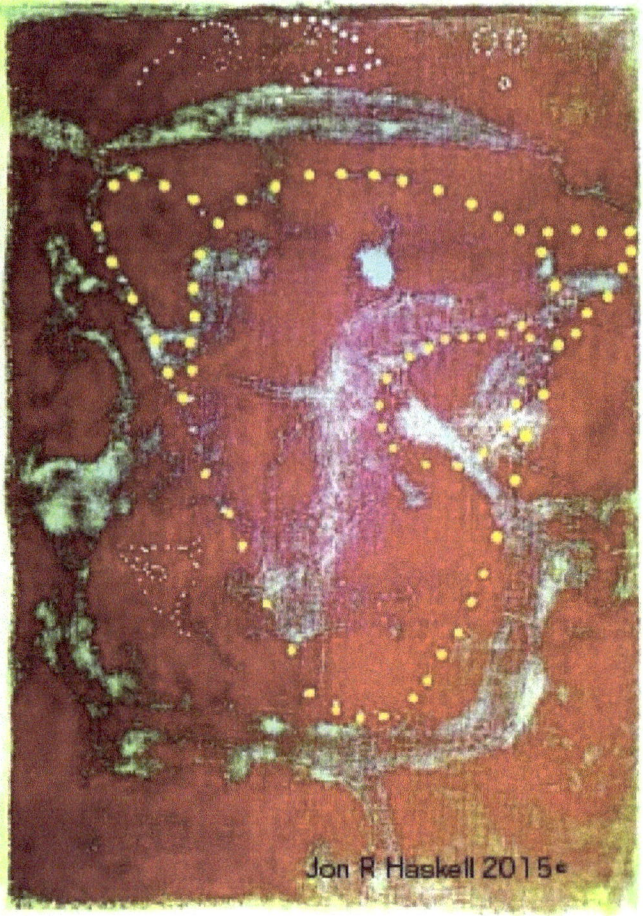

Fig 92, Monochromatic silk painting, Man Riding on a Dragon 3rd BCE, from www.wikipedia.org

Fig 93, Color stretched image Man Riding on a Dragon 3rd C BCE showing dragon and bird motifs, from www.wikipedia.org, by author

Left center is the head of a long serpentine dragon version that flows to the opposite side of the canvas, and in the center is the faint outline of another dragon face with the distinctive pointed eye.

Another example of the two motifs appearing as subtle background art can be seen in the silk painting from the Song Dynasty some 900 years later in time.

Fig. 94, Color stretched image with partially traced bird and dragons, Song Dynasty 960-1368 CE, from wikipedia.org, by author

To summarize, the China examples cover the period from the Paleolithic Period thru the Song Dynasty ending in 1368 CE.

North America Examples in Chronological Order

The motifs seem to appear in North America during the Upper Paleolithic Period (c 40,000- c 10,000 BCE). The oldest examples found come from the Topper site in South Carolina where radiocarbon dating produced results dated to over 50,000 years (figures 95 & 96))

Despite their age, the motif's style and conventions are generally consistent with other much later in time examples. The exception to this is the dragon tails do not appear to curve to the left, but extend downward from the face with two straight converging lines.

Examples continue with other pre-Clovis artifacts and then move forward in time using artifacts from eastern North America from the Paleo-Eskimo Dorset thru Mississippian cultures.

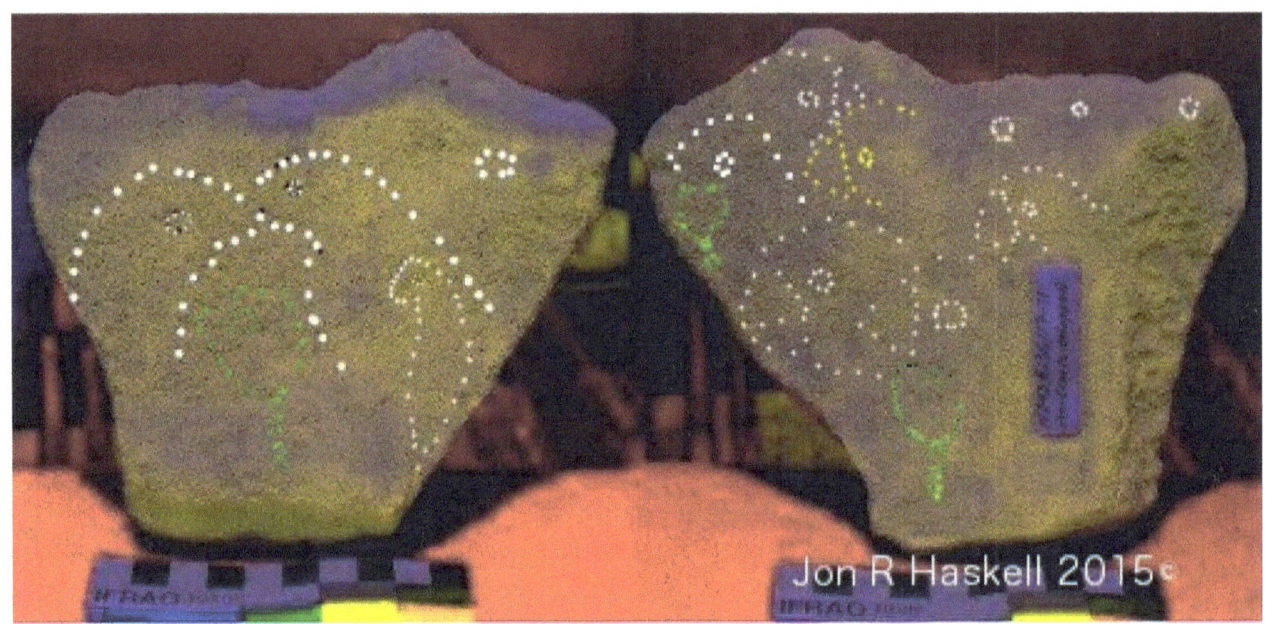

Fig. 95. Color modified image of lithic tool, Topper Site, South Carolina, from figurestones.blogspot.com, by author

Fig. 96, Color modified image of lithic tool, Topper site, South Carolina, from www.ishtargate.com, by author

The Meadowcroft rock shelter has an extensive amount of imagery which were quite easily identifiable because of prominent tool marks. Unfortunately no high-resolution pictures of lithic material suitable for tracings could be located.

Fig. 97, Meadowcroft escarpment showing birds and dragon, photo by Darrell Mintz, color stretched image and tracings by author

The Clovis examples in the following graphics are from the Gault site in Texas and Cactus Hill located in Virginia. The quantity of small and detailed motifs was surprising, particularly the large example in figure 99. The tool marks identifying the upper and lower parrot beak on two small birds are anatomically exacting using evenly spaced tool marks (figures 98 A, B)

There are a series of 10 double line features, partially outlined in red that traverse the width of the piece which form 9 segmented sections. While it may be coincidental, these may represent the Chinese convention of segmenting dragon tails in multiples of nine.

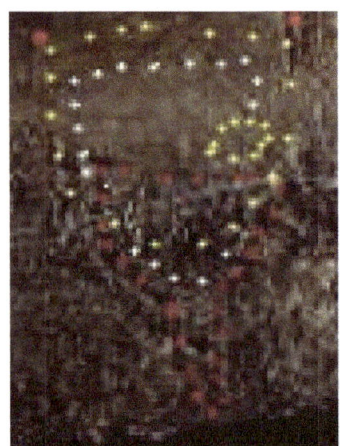

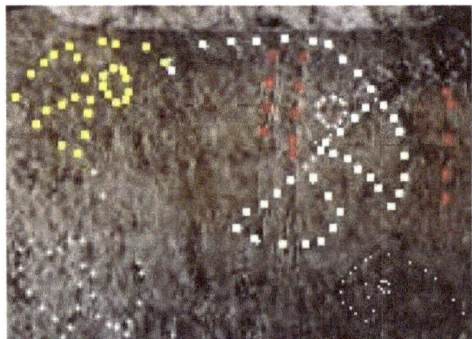

Fig. 98 A & b, Close view of larger artifact in 96, by author

Fig. 99, Gault site Clovis artifacts with partial tracings of bird and dragon motifs, from www.lithiccastinglab.com, by author

Fig. 100, Bird and dragon motifs on bird shaped lithic artifacts, Gualt site, Texas, from Gault Archeological Project, by author

The small bird on the Cactus Hill artifact with two well defined tail feathers is one of only two that could be traced with certainty and differs from the normally seen one tail feather depiction. This is noteworthy because in the Fenghuang pair, the two tail bird represents the feminine bird and the one tail bird is the male. This pairing is clearly illustrated at the Upper Falls at Hocking Hills in Ohio (figure 102) where they appear at a crevice.

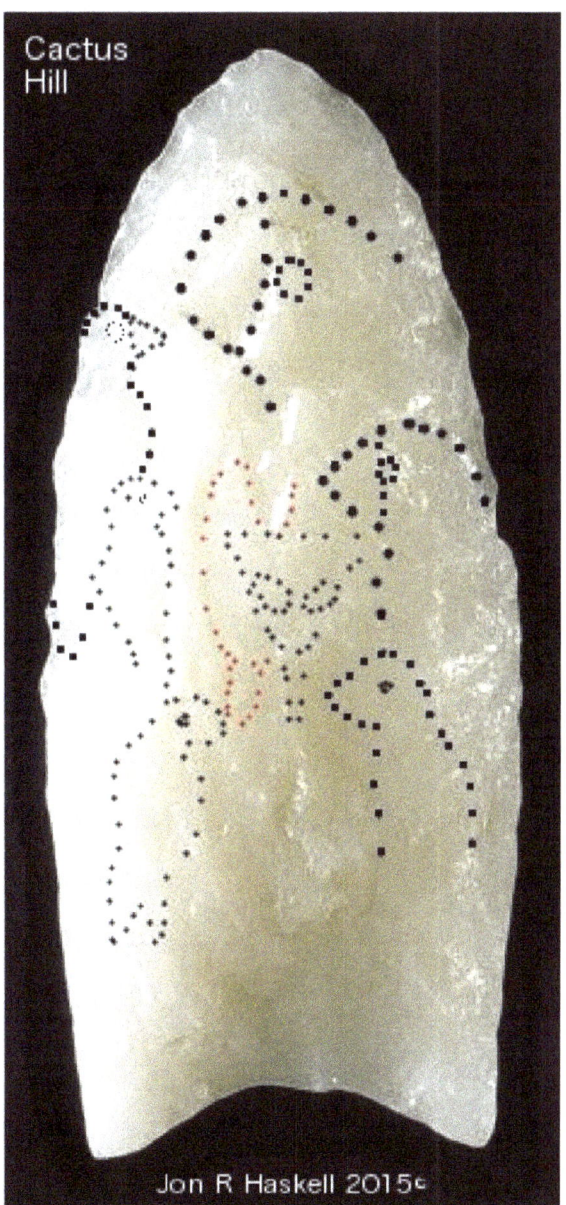

Fig. 101, Cactus Hill site, Virginia, from unknown internet source, tracings by author

Fig. 102, Bird with two tail feathers

This artifact is one of twenty four from the Salish peoples village of Temixwten, British Columbia in Western Canada which are dated from 7,500 to 3,000 BCE[4]. Described as a Charm, this small piece yielded discernible tool marks for tracing.

Though it was visually suggested in other examples reviewed, the tripartite crown, the authority symbol of a Chinese emperor, is prominently featured on this artifact. Tracings suggest there are two crowns suggesting two face figures occupying the space.

The website featuring these artifacts provides well documented information regarding the association of these examples to counterparts from Northeast Asia and the cultural ties of the ancestors of the Salish to that region.

Fig. 103 showing bird-pair motif, dragon and bird eyes, from http://www.temixwten.net, tracings by author

Fig.104, Alternate view of figure 86 showing face with tri-partite head dress and other motifs, from http://www.temixwten.net, tracings by author

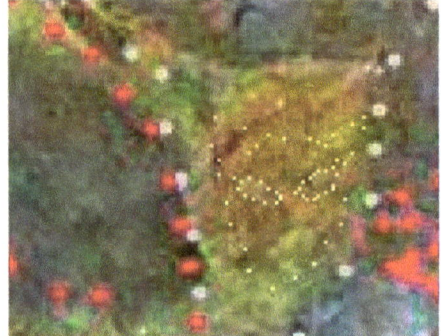

Fig. 105, Close view of traced dragon face, by author

---

4 Bruce Brown, www.temixwten.net

This example is from the Dorset Culture who migrated from Alaska to northeast Canada which includes Baffin Island, Labrador and western Greenland.

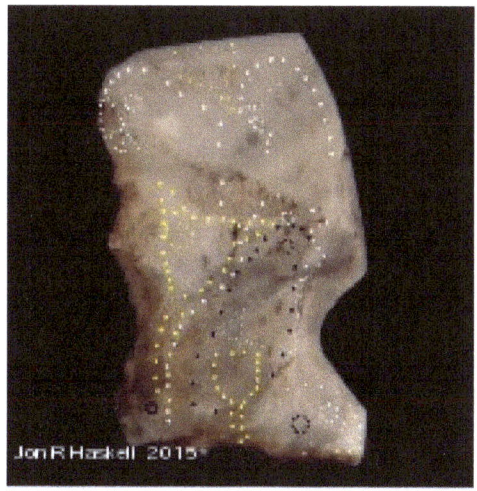 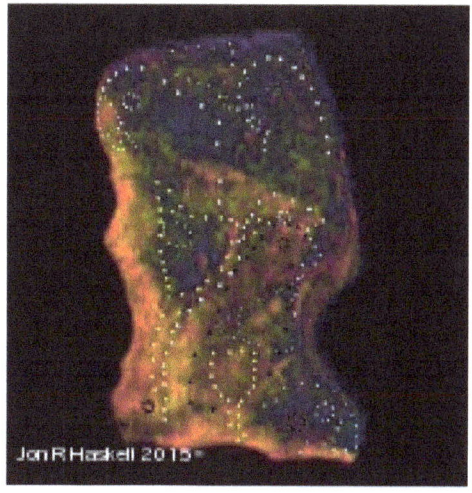

Figs. 106 & 107, Burin-Like Tool, Dorset Paleo Eskimo, 2500-1000 BCE approx., from www.archaeowiki.com, by author

Further south, the Glacial Kame culture (c3000-500 BCE)) occupied lands in northwest Ohio and some areas of adjacent states and the southern portion of Ontario Province Canada.

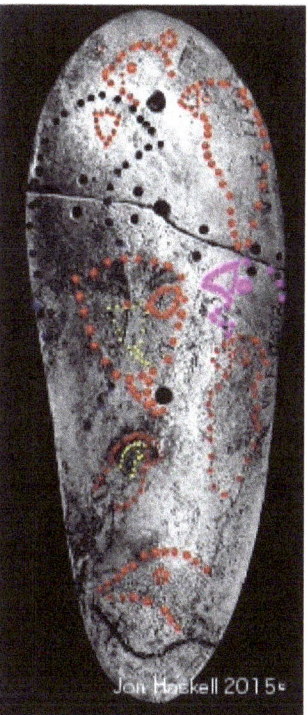

Fig. 108, Glacial Kame broken sandal-sole shell gorget, Ontario Canada, Cunningham 1948, by author

Further south along the Ohio River and later in time, the motifs continue on Adena artifacts. On the "pants" of the character in figure 109 is what I interpret as two serpentine dragons, each with a face and one with a tail terminating in a triangular tip. The perimeter of the pants and hips along with the red outlined eye, could also be reasonably interpreted as another dragon face.

The outline of the pants and hips and the red outlined large eye form another dragon-face. The two dark spots on the pants, navel area and head (figure 99) are also dragon motifs. As mentioned earlier, many examples have these dark areas on and around the dragon motif. This maybe related to a apatite crystal glaze found on some of the Temixwten artifacts from British Columbia. Conflated with the serpentine form are a number of elongated bird heads and numerous other scattered bird motifs.

Fig 109, Color modified close view of Adena Pipe, showing bird and dragon motifs, from apps.ohiohistory.org, by author

Fig. 110, Adena Pipe, from The Ohio Historical Society

Fig. 111, Adena pipe with dragon and bird motifs, from www.ohiohistory.org, by author

Following the Adena Culture the Scioto (Ohio) Hopewell Culture (100-500 BCE) emerged with a culture and a way of life that spread to other groups thru out much of eastern and central North America.

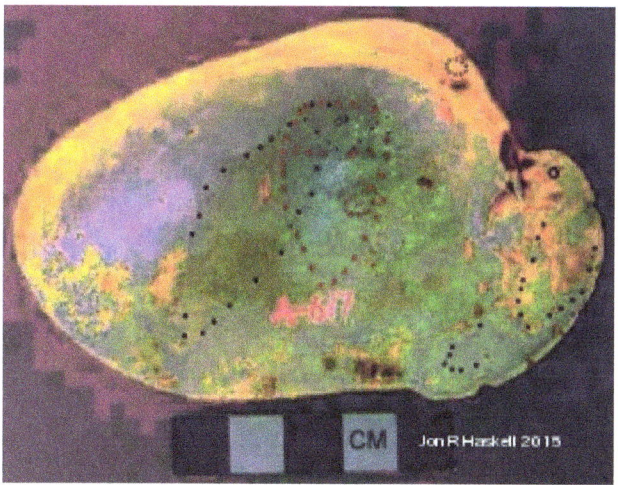

Fig. 112, Color Hopewell shell spoon, Turner Mound Group, Ohio, color stretched image, from pmem.unix.fas.harvard.edu, by author

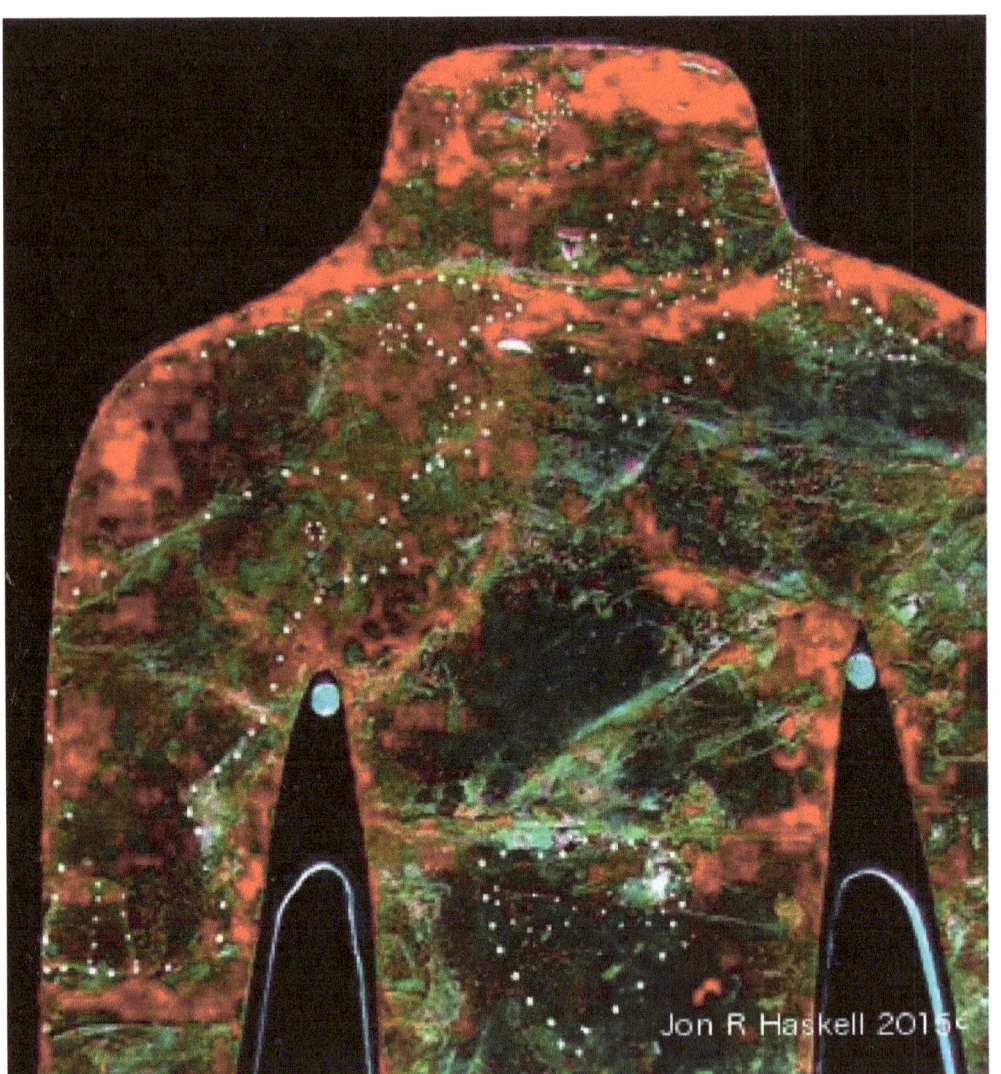 

Fig. 113, Hopewell Mica Figure, color stretched image with bird and dragon motifs, from www.ohiohistory.org, by author

Following Hopewell is the Mississippian Culture (800-1600 CE) in the midwest and southeast part of North America. I have chosen a personal favorite, the Birdman Tablet from the Cahokia archeological site along the Mississippi River. It is an complex piece saturated with small imagery, some of which are two small to trace without distorting the figure. One of these small figures is interpreted as face with feathered head dress which noted by the arrow in figure 103.

The small imagery also appears on the pectoral where at least two dragons are located with the larger carved face outline having features resembling horns. Surrounding the pectoral, are four birds (not traced), two with heads at the bottom facing inward. Just above the dragon eyes is another bird (not traced) with its triangular beak facing toward the pectoral.

Figs. 114 & 115 Birdman Tablet, Cahokia, with motifs, from wikipedia commons, by author

Western Europe-France

The final example in this chronology section is an artifact from the Solutrean culture (c19,000 BCE) from Ice Age Europe. This was a surprising find which seems to support the Solutrean hypothesis which contends that Europeans were in the Americas prior to the migration of peoples from Asia known as the Clovis culture (c 11,500 BCE)

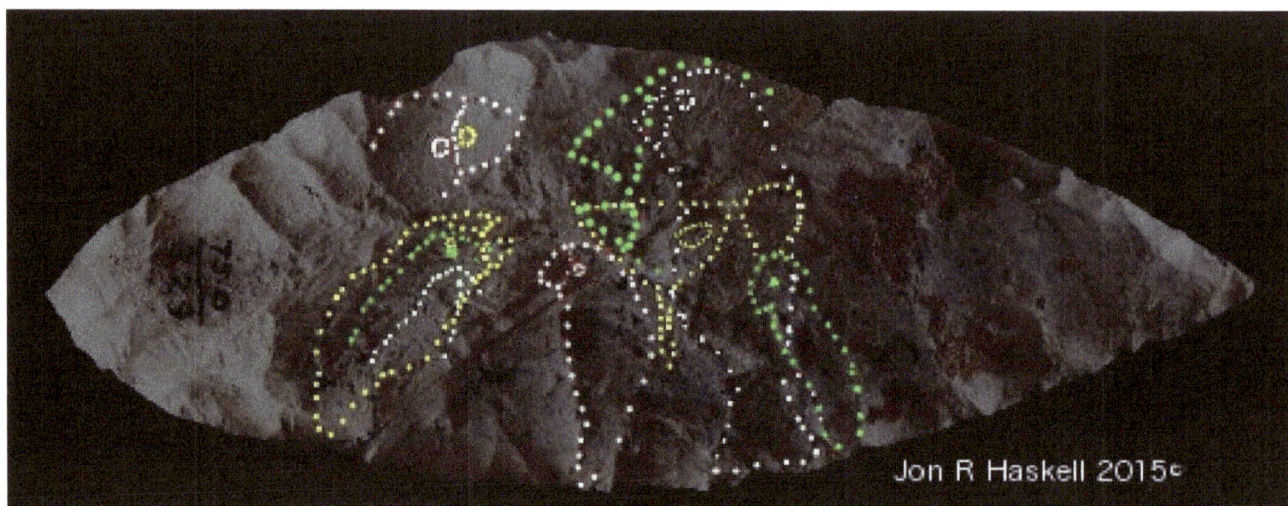

Fig. 116, Solutrean lithic tool, from www.lithicastinglab.com, tracings by author

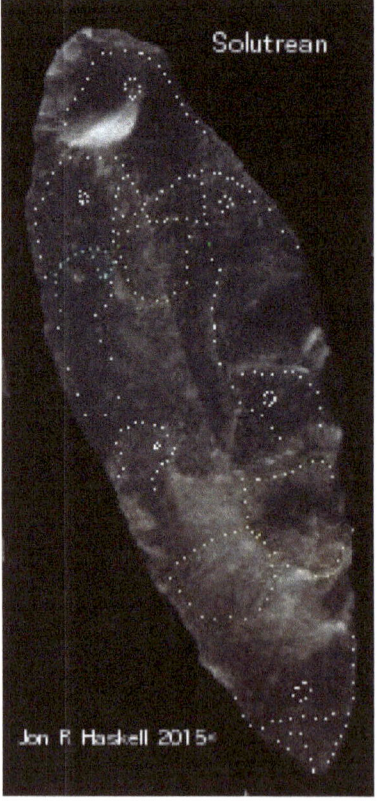

Fig. 117, Solutrean lithic, from unknown internet source, by author

Controversial Artifacts

This section presents several artifacts which have been the subject of much debate since their discovery during the 19th and 20th centuries.

On close inspection of the Decalogue stone, the bulbous features on the backwards facing "E" shaped script have small incised "eyes" anatomically placed giving the appearance of a bird's head.

Based upon the presence of the two motifs on the artifacts in this section and the remote probability a fraudster would know of the motifs, it is my opinion that they are legitimate artifacts and the debate over their authenticity is resolved.

Fig. 118 Newark Decalogue Stone, Newark, Ohio, from en.wikipedia.org, tracings by author.

Fig. 119, Newark Holy Stone, from www.econ.ohio-state.edu, color modified image and tracings by author.

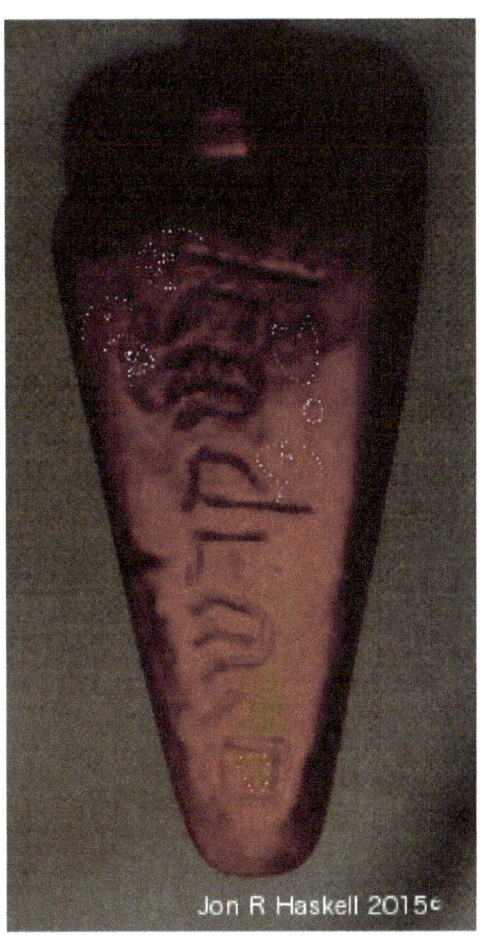

Fig.120, Bat Creek Stone, Tennessee, from www.ascensionearth2012.org, tracings by author

Fig. 121 & 122, Kensington Rune Stone, Minnesota, from www.kensingtonrunestone.us, color stretched image and tracings by author

Conclusion

What started as a serendipitous encounter with unfamiliar rock art in northern Georgia rapidly morphed into an intellectually addictive global search for the origin and mythological meaning of the two motifs. Little did I realize at the start, that the motifs extended so deep into human history and were so globally prolific. As an initial foray into what evolved into a complex subject, it produced a myriad of questions and ramifications related to the peopling, cultural development and mythologies of North American indigenous groups.

The by whom and from what direction the motifs arrived in North America questions seems to have multiple answers depending on the time period. From the east, we have seen the motif trail extend from the Solutrean Culture (ca 19,000-15,000 BCE) of western Europe to pre-Clovis sites (ca 14,000 BCE) in eastern America. This on the surface seems to supports the Solutrean hypothesis.

To the west, we have the motifs on artifacts from the Paleolithic Laonainaimiao site in Henan Province China, home of the first recorded dynasty, the 21st BCE century Xia Dynasty. Though not shown in this paper, the motifs can be seen extending from Henan Province into far north east Asia leading to the Bering crossing augmenting the Bering approach.

The long studied similarity of the art and mythologies of the Mesoamerican Olmec (1500-400 BCE) to Chinese counterparts are also supported with the sculpted heads from Chavin de Huantar whose 1500 BCE dating seems hardly coincidental. Around 900 BCE, the Olmec concepts of rulership, social stratification, along with their iconography and mythology spread to other Mesoamerican groups who modified them to meet their local needs. With this in mind, it is not unreasonable to speculate that the feathered serpent theme of Mesoamerican and North American symbolism and deities are the result of conflating the dragon and the phoenix into a singular form.

There are numerous directions for future research. One of particular interest is though the two motifs stylistically remained generally unchanged over time, in retrospect there were subtle differences in the dragon motif. The shape of the head varied with chevron, skull and oval shapes. The pointed slanted eye cartouche has several different shapes and their inclination varied. Other eyes seemed to be oval shaped with little or no inclination. Some motifs have no evidence of horns or wings, others had mushroom shaped, curved, pointed and triangular forms. Are these a result of artistic liberty, or does it indicate temporal related changes or a regional/cultural preference?

Because the change in the form of the Chinese dragon is well documented, it may be possible to isolate the dragon motif variations by time and region. As an example, when the Shang Dynasty conquered the Xia Dynasty who used the dragon as their totem, the Shang so respected the Xia they incorporated the dragon with their phoenix totem, and added one horn.

Closing on a personal note, this research has been an exciting voyage of discovery and has confirmed my belief that it necessary to look outside North America to fully understand it's long and complex history. There is much to be learned and I hope this paper's topic will foster additional research by others.

Jon R. Haskell, Indigenous Peoples Research Foundation ©2015